WE HOPE YOU AND YOUR LOVED ONES NEVER NEED THIS BOOK— BUT IF YOU DO, THERE IS NO BETTER BOOK TO HAVE.

Whether the first aid emergency is as minor as a small burn or as major as a massive heart attack,

as outwardly induced as a bee-sting or as inwardly induced as an emotional breakdown,

as seemingly simple as a cut or as frighteningly bewildering as a drug overdose or the DTs,

as annoying as a speck in the eye or as agonizing as a broken bone,

as varied as a sports injury, an auto accident, and an emergency birth,

this long-needed guide will tell you what you need to know exactly when you need to know it, precisely how to do what you have to do, and everything else essential to save you from the feelings of helplessness and hopelessness ~~that can lead to a misery~~ ssible disaster.

There is no better

D1432636

FIRST AID WITHOUT PANIC

by Joel Hartley M.D., F.A.C.S.

Illustrations by Nancy Gahan

POPULAR LIBRARY . NEW YORK

POPULAR LIBRARY EDITION

May, 1977

Copyright (c) 1975 Hart Publishing Company, Inc.

Library of Congress Catalog Card Number: 74-27696
Published by arrangement with Hart Publishing Co., Inc.

ISBN: 0-445-08603-3

*To my dear wife, Freddie,
always so very helpful*

PRINTED IN THE UNITED STATES OF AMERICA

CONTENTS

Basic Information

Emergencies

INDEX   367

INTRODUCTION

A little over five years ago, my wife and I were visiting Africa. Along with another tourist, we had chartered a twin-motored Commanche to fly us to the Ngorongoro Crater in Tanzania. We were flying over an isolated animal preserve when our small craft got caught in thick fog and a sudden downdraft. In an instant, we crashed into the side of a mountain. Needless to say, immediate medical assistance was out of the question.

The pilot had suffered severe hemorrhaging, lacerations of the forehead and nose, and a fracture of the nasal bone. My spine and ribs were fractured. The other passenger had been similarly maltreated; only my wife escaped with less than serious effects. Alone in that wilderness, dazed and shocked, and with our radio broken, things looked rather bleak.

It has been my practice for 40 years to carry along with me, no matter where I go, a first aid kit. And in the situation in which we found ourselves, it was that first aid kit that saved the day. Though partially disabled, I was still able to stop the bleeding, splint and bandage the victims, and administer sedatives.

After six hours, we finally managed to reach a road and were picked up by a Land Rover of one of the tourist lodges. Eventually, we received full medical attention, but it was the prompt first aid that was responsible for no one's being permanently damaged.

When Mr. Hart learned about the story, he was very much impressed, and he asked me to write a book on first aid. During our discussions, it became evident that many of the first aid procedures which I had learned as an intern had long since been superseded, and that brand new techniques had been developed even during the last five years. So many formerly well-entrenched practices had gone by the board. It seemed to me that it was not enough just to write a book about first aid; what needed publication were the new techniques and the new ways of treatment that had developed. And so, during the preparation of this book, I repeatedly consulted specialists to make sure this volume would, indeed, reflect the very latest treatments and techniques.

Another matter cropped up in our discussions. It appeared that most first aid books assumed that when an emergency occurred, the first-aider would have all the time in the world to wade through a manual to find what he was looking for. This is unrealistic. When an accident occurs, there is generally much excitement. The plain fact is that in certain cases, unless swift measures are taken, the victim will die or suffer permanent injury.

For example, if a baby swallows poison, is there time for the first-aider to plow through a large body of small type to find out what to do? While all this reading is going on, the baby might be lost.

It became our set conviction that all first aid

directives should be terse, and that the type should be large. Accordingly, in this volume bold headings guide the first-aider directly—via the shortest possible route—to the information he is seeking.

A paramount goal has been to simplify the text. Let it be emphasized that this book has been written for laymen. Latin names and even fairly well-known medical terms have been avoided in favor of common idiom.

Finally, let me point out that just about every page in this volume emphasizes that the recommended treatment is only an emergency treatment, and that medical assistance should be promptly sought.

I should like to express my thanks to those colleagues who have so generously helped me in preparing certain sections of this handbook. I should also like particularly to express my thanks to the artist, Nancy Gahan, and to her husband, Tony Gahan, who were so painstaking in their endeavors to translate my directives with exactitude. They both were wonderfully cooperative and extremely patient.

Joel Hartley, M.D.

HOW TO USE
THIS BOOK

This manual is comprised of two sections. The first section explains basic materials and procedures in first aid treatment. Here you will find a discussion of such things as band-aids, ampoules, and crutches. Here also you will find a complete discussion on such matters as how to feel a pulse, how to bandage a wound, how to apply a tourniquet, etc.

It is suggested that the reader who really wants to acquire a knowledge of first aid read and study these basic procedures at home and at leisure *before* an emergency arises in which such techniques will be required. Though every effort has been made to render these explanations simple in the extreme, it is nevertheless true that when an accident occurs, there is generally too much excitement and rarely enough time for a first-aider to study and acquaint himself with exact techniques. Therefore, a perusal and a reperusal of these sections—perhaps, even a few readings—followed by a little home practice in bandaging will prove to be extremely rewarding when the first-aider is actually faced with the necessity of applying these techniques. In the case of bandaging, it is recommended that the first-aider work with a partner, so that actual practice can be obtained.

The second section of this book deals with specific injuries or accidents or untoward happenings, such as a bee sting, a broken thigh, or swallowing of poison by an infant. Here the treatment is telescoped to the reader in concise directives. The essentials of treatment are set forth in proper sequence. If there is more than one thing that should be done, then each step is numbered.

Under each subject, the statement of treatment is followed by an expanded discussion under the heading *What the Doctor Says*. The first-aider need not read these comments at a time when he is addressing himself to an emergency treatment. The main thing is to administer aid to the victim as promptly as possible. But after the essential steps have been taken, the first-aider can get pertinent additional information by reading the highly informative supplemental comment.

All injuries and emergency situations are arranged in this book alphabetically. If you don't find what you are looking for, look in the index for what strikes you as the key word in the injury. For example, somebody may have been hit on the head with a club, and may be lying bleeding. You are the only one around to help. The words you may think of may be "hit on the head" or "injury" or "bleeding from head." If you look up any of these in the index, you will be referred to the section in this book entitled HEAD INJURY.

A number of diseases are known by different names. For example, diarrhea is also called dysentery, and is popularly known as "the runs." If you looked up any of these words in the index you would be referred to the proper page, for the index lists *most* likely names.

Similarly, if a person were stung by an insect, you might think of "insect stings," or "stings," or "insect bites." These three listings would be found in the index, and you would be referred to the chapter on STINGS OF INSECTS.

BASIC
INFORMATION

HOW TO HANDLE AN EMERGENCY

In case of an accident

1. Speak to the victim and to the persons at the scene to find out what happened.

2. Be calm and reassuring.

3. Examine the victim from head to toe. *See page 22.*

4. Determine the simplest and most direct form of action. Look up the section in this book containing the necessary instructions. *See page 16* on HOW TO USE THIS BOOK.

5. Do not rush to move the victim.

6. Do not give the victim water.

7. Do not give the victim alcohol.

8. Do only what you are sure is correct. If you are not reasonably sure, take no action at all. Hasty or improper action may do harm and may cause irreparable injury.

OVERVIEW OF EMERGENCY SITUATION

First things first

Upon arriving at the scene of an emergency, the first-aider should immediately observe the surroundings, and if possible, obtain from the victim or from an observer an account of what has happened. Next, quickly determine the following, and take any necessary action. Is there evidence of:

1. Breathing *See page 99*.

2. Bleeding (laceration, gunshot wound, open fracture) *See page 47*.

3. Consciousness *See page 358*.

4. Pulse *See page 42*.

5. Shock *See page 334*.

6. Head injury *See page 287*.

7. Foreign body in the windpipe *See page 115*.

8. Chemical in the eye *See page 202*.

9. Thermal or chemical burn *See page 154*.

10. Electrocution or the effects of lightning *See pages 196 and 301.*

11. Heart attack, stroke, diabetic coma, or insulin shock *See pages 289, 350, 184, and 298.*

12. Ingested poison *See page 317.*

13. Sucking wound of the chest *See page 162.*

14. Poisoning by smoke or noxious fumes *See page 307.*

15. Anaphylactic shock due to insect bite or injected drug *See pages 28 and 343.*

16. Imminent explosion in the surrounding area *See page 87.*

17. Snakebite *See page 139.*

The above list includes virtually all the conditions one might encounter that would require prompt action on the scene.

After completing this rapid survey and taking any necessary immediate action, perform a quick general physical examination from head to toe, as outlined below.

If in doubt, take no action, but arrange for further assistance.

Examining the Victim

Without being a doctor or a nurse, an intelligent individual can perform a quick, general and systematic examination of the entire body of the victim, starting at the head and proceeding rapidly to the toes. This examination can be done without doing any damage to the victim. Within a few minutes, an amazing fund of information can be obtained. Based upon this information, the first-aider can make his judgment on what course of action should be taken. He should be able to make an intelligent report to a physician.

Once you have rapidly checked the 17 conditions listed above, you should proceed to examine the victim more closely:

Gently feel the victim's skull—the front, the back, and the sides. Are there any depressions in the bones? Is there any bleeding from the scalp? *See page 271.*

Is there any bleeding from the ears, nose or mouth?

Is the victim suffering from any injuries to his eyes? Look at the lids. Gently open the lids and look at the eyeballs. Are they intact? Are the pupils equal in size? Is either or both pupils widely dilated, or contracted to a pinpoint? Do the pupils contract when you shine a bright light at them (as they should)? *See page 109.*

Feel the neck. Is there any pain in this region? Perform *very slight* and *very gentle* motion of the neck by bending the head ever so slightly forward and rotating the head gently from side to side. Note if there is any complaint of pain. Before shifting the victim's position, be sure that you will not harm him by doing so. This is especially important in a case where you suspect that the victim's neck might be broken.

Does the victim have a wound on the chest? If so, see text on *page 162*, and *Figure 80 on page 164*; these describe the handling of penetrating wounds of the chest.

Does the victim experience pain on gentle compression of the chest? If so, this may indicate fractured ribs. *See page 266*.

Does breathing in and out cause the victim to complain of pain in the chest?

Touch each upper extremity from the shoulder to the finger tips. *Be gentle*. Move the shoulder slightly by rotating and bending it. Does the victim experience pain? If so, try to localize the pain. Is the pain in the wrist or in the shoulder or in the elbow, or in between these regions? Are there any deformities of the upper extremities?

Is the victim suffering from abdominal pain? Are there any wounds on the abdomen? Keep in mind that a sharp instrument may make a very small puncture wound in the abdomen, yet cause severe internal damage.

Are the muscles of the abdomen held tight? Is the abdomen rigid?

Are there any bullet wounds visible on the body? *Do not hesitate to cut off clothing rapidly to examine an injured part*. Such procedure is both faster and safer than removing the victim's clothes.

Has the victim sustained a pelvic fracture? To determine, press both sides of the pelvis inward to detect any pain. *See Figure 120 on page 264*, and text on *page 264*.

Touch and gently move the lower extremities from

the hips to the toes. This will help you to find out the source of the pain. Does any part of this area show a deformity? Are there any wounds?

Run your hand up and down the victim's spine from top to bottom, from the back of the neck to the tail bone. The presence of pain may indicate a bruise, a wound, or a possible fracture.

Can the victim speak?

Is the victim able to move his arms and legs voluntarily?

Is there any evidence of burns due to heat, or chemicals, or electricity?

Are there any signs of shock? If so, *see page 334.*

Is there any evidence of convulsions? *See page 181.*

After this rapid inspection, you will have collected enough facts on which to base an intelligent judgment of what, if any, first aid is required. Specific instructions covering each situation are set forth in the pages of this manual.

A last word on general emergency procedure: don't refrain from administering first aid solely out of fear that you will become involved in a legal fracas with the victim or the victim's family. If your impulse is to be a Good Samaritan, then in my view you should act on your impulse. To date, 41 states have enacted "Good Samaritan" laws which absolve the first aider of responsibility for malpractice or neglect in an emergency situation. But law or no law, don't let someone suffer or die merely because you don't want to "get involved."

Learn the basic first aid techniques presented in this first part of the book, and you will be prepared to save the life or ease the pain of a fellow human being.

DISEASE EMBLEM

A person with a medical problem should take means to have his failing made known to any first-aider or doctor who may be obliged to treat him at some time. Such a person should wear an identification emblem on which is described the disease from which he is suffering, or a notification of which drugs will be helpful to him, which drugs he may be allergic to, and what his blood type is. This information will be of great benefit to the persons who are treating him and may result in the avoidance of a possibly fatal error in his treatment.

An organization known as MEDIC ALERT FOUNDA-TION INTERNATIONAL maintains headquarters at Turlock, California 95380. The telephone number is 209-632-2371. For a small fee, this organization will supply any person with a bracelet or neck pendant which bears the information described above.

This identification label should be worn constantly on the body. MEDIC ALERT maintains a central file at its headquarters with detailed medical information about each individual who has registered with it, the address of the physician who has treated such a person in the past, and the address of the nearest relative of such a person.

Should a person registered with MEDIC ALERT become incapacitated or be in a situation where he is unable to offer full information to the attending physician, the emblem will alert the first-aider or the attending physician that more detailed information about the patient can be obtained from the central files of MEDIC ALERT. This information is available 24 hours a day and can be obtained through a collect telephone call.

The information that should be engraved on the bracelet or pendant should indicate that the patient is:

1. An arthritic taking cortisone or ACTH.

2. A cardiac taking digitalis or some other drug.

3. A diabetic.

4. An epileptic.

5. A sufferer from hemophilia or purpura.

6. A sufferer from myasthenia gravis.

7. A sufferer from glaucoma.

8. A wearer of contact lenses.

9. A particular blood type.

The American Medical Association now issues medical identification cards available to patients who have special health problems. On such cards there can be noted the information needed by any first-aider who helps the patient during an accident or during some sudden illness. These cards are available to doctors, or at a very low cost they can be ordered from the A.M.A. Order Handling Unit at 535 North Dearborn Street, Chicago, Illinois 60610.

These cards will fit any wallet. *See Figure 1.*

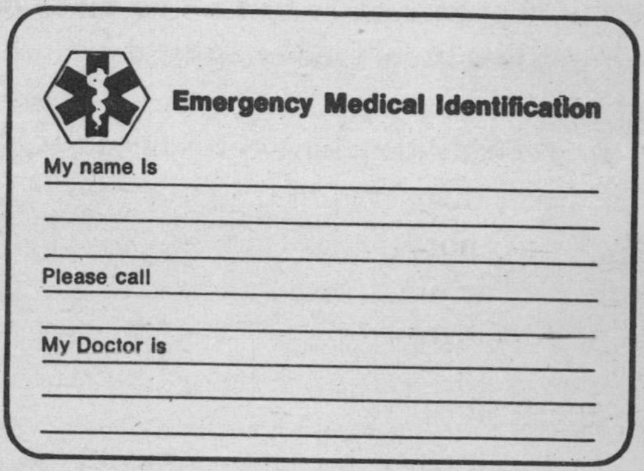

FIG. 1 *WALLET CARD This emergency medical identification is issued by the American Medical Association.*

FIRST AID KIT

A first aid kit should conform to the requirements of expected use. For example, a first aid kit that would be useful at home would be somewhat different from a first aid kit which is taken along on a camping expedition to an isolated area. Moreover, certain persons, because of individual need, may require unusual items which ordinarily would not be included in a first aid kit. For example, a diabetic might need insulin and a supply of syringes for self-injection.

Any special medications should be clearly labeled. The container should also state the dose and the directions for use, so that if the person for whom the medication is intended should become disabled in any way, the drug can be administered correctly by someone else.

The variety of first aid items and the amount of the supplies will, of course, vary with the number of people for whom the kit will serve. A physician, of course, is best qualified to offer such advice. For general use, a first aid kit should consist of the following items:

1. Sterile gauze pads, large and small.

2. Roll of gauze bandage.

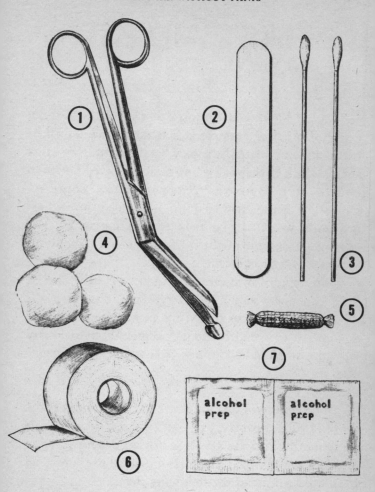

FIG. 2   SOME MATERIALS AND INSTRUMENTS USED
IN FIRST AID   (1) Bandage scissors. (2) Tongue depressor. (3)
Cotton-tipped applicators. (4) Cotton balls. (5) Ampoule of Spirits of
Ammonia. (6) Adhesive tape. (7) Alcohol pad enclosed in sealed envelope.

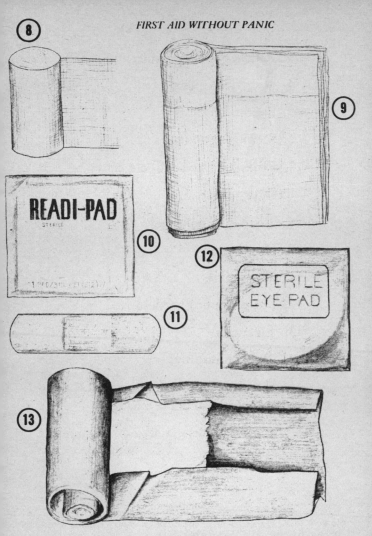

(8) Roller gauze bandage. (9) Multi-layered gauze. (10) Sterile gauze pad
in prepared container. (11) Band-aid. (12) Sterile eye pad in prepared
container. (13) Roll of absorbent cotton.

3. Band-aids, both regular and Telfa*

4. Adhesive tape.

5. Bandage scissors.

6. Sterile cotton balls.

7. Roll of sterile absorbent cotton.

8. Safety razors.

9. Triangular bandages.

10. Mouth gag.

11. Safety pins.

12. Cotton-tipped applicators.

13. Tweezers.

14. Plastic measuring cup.

15. Ampoule of Spirits of Ammonia.** (smelling salts - ammonia inhalant).

16. Aspirin tablets 300 mg. in strength (5 grains).

*Telfa—Trade name for non-adherent dressing. Supplied by Kendall Co., Bauer & Black Division. There are other good non-adherent dressings supplied by other manufacturers.

**Vaporole—Aromatic Ammonia. Burroughs, Wellcome Co.

17. Darvon capsules*; this is a non-narcotic pain relieving medication, 32 milligrams (1/2 grain). These tablets are stronger than aspirin and may be combined with aspirin.

18. Hydrogen peroxide.

19. Antibiotic ointment (*Neosporin, Bacimycin* or *Furacin*).

20. Soap. A cake of plain white soap or *Dial* soap containing hexachlorophene. Liquid antiseptic soap such as the hexachlorophenes, *Physohex* or *Septisol*, or the iodofor soap, *Betadyne*, will also be useful.

21. Elastic bandage. This comes in widths of two inches (5 centimeters), three inches (7.5 centimeters), four inches (10 centimeters), and six inches (15 centimeters). The three-inch width is serviceable for most purposes.

22. Tourniquet (heavy piece of cloth such as canvas, ½ inch (1 to 2 centimeters) wide and 36 inches (90 centimeters) long.

*Eli Lilly, Indianapolis, Indiana 46206.

EXPANDED FIRST AID KIT

In any situation where it is known in advance that medical aid will not be readily available, an expanded first aid kit should be prepared to handle plausible emergency situations. When a group goes out hunting or hiking in the woods, or when a group takes a trip of exploration into an uninhabited area, preparations should be more sophisticated. The leader of the group should familiarize himself with available medical services and supplies in the area, as well as the location of radio or phone communication, ambulance service, and airplane ambulance service.

The same holds true where an industrial unit is established in a remote territory, and may also be true in any factory where the nature of the machines in use render it likely that an accident of a serious nature may occur that requires more elaborate materials for handling on-the-spot first aid.

In such an expanded first aid kit, all of the items mentioned in this section, as well as all those in the smaller first aid kit, *see page 31*, should be included. However, quantities of materials and medication should be increased to handle possible need.

1. Gauze or universal dressing, 10 inches by 9 inches (25 cms. by 22.5 cms.). The universal dressing comes packed and ready to use.

2. Butterfly bandages.

3. Alcohol wipettes.

4. Plastic air splints. *See page 89*.

5. Padded wooden splints. *See page 80*.

6. Activated charcoal tablets. Used for poisoning cases. Can be obtained at any pharmacy.

7. Syrup of Ipecac, 4 teaspoons (15 cc.). To stimulate vomiting in poisoning cases.

8. Sterile razor or scalpel (for snake bites requiring incision at point of penetration of the fangs). (In an emergency the use of non-sterile instruments would be permitted.)

9. Sterile cotton applicators.

10. Sterile eye pads.

11. Eyecup.

12. Paper cups.

13. Pencil and pad.

14. Flashlight.

15. Sterile tongue depressors.

16. Short board splint for neck injuries. *See Figure 3.*

17. Long board splint for spinal injuries. *See Figure 4.*

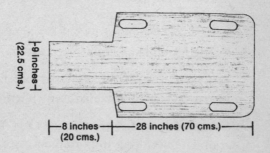

FIG. 3 *SHORT BOARD Use for transporting a victim with fracture of neck or upper spine.*

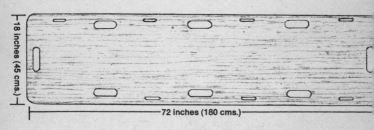

FIG. 4 *LONG BOARD Use for transporting a victim with fracture of the back.*

The following medications should be included in an expanded first aid kit where the first-aider has been given actual instruction in their use by a physician. The person who presumes to use these medications should be aware of their consequences and should have reliable knowledge on how to administer these drugs. These drugs can only be obtained through a physician's prescription. Such a prescription should be accompanied by special instruction as to how the drugs should be used, on whom they should be used, and in what emergency situations they should be used. These drugs are:

1. Codeine sulfate, ¼ grain (15 milligrams) tablets, for pain.

2. Phenobarbital, ¼ grain (15 milligrams) for sedation.

3. Antibiotics.

4. Snake antivenin serum.

The leader of the group is advised to take the following precaution: For each person in your group write down the names of the drugs to which he is allergic. This should be done in advance of the trip. Asking for such information at the time when an emergency occurs may result in receiving garbled and inaccurate information, and the victim of an accident may be seriously hurt through the administration of drugs which he never should have been given.

If an expedition enters an area where poisonous snakes are known to exist, it would be wise to have on hand antivenin serum. Be sure, in such a case, to have full medical instructions for use on hand before the expedition enters the area.

FIG. 5 *REMOVING STERILE ALCOHOL PAD FROM CONTAINER* *The sterile pad can be easily removed from the container by just tearing open the corner of the package. It is best to eliminate unnecessary handling of the pad before it is used for antiseptic cleansing of the skin area. Do not apply this pad on an open wound. This will cause an extreme burning sensation.*

When a group is in an isolated area where medical facilities are not available, and where, without ministration, the patient's health may be seriously impaired, the layman may be justified in taking more extensive action than he would prudently take where medical facilities were in range.

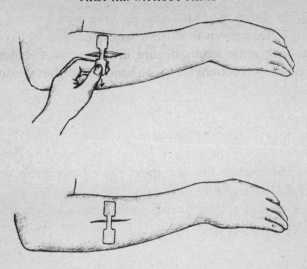

FIG. 6 *BUTTERFLY BANDAGE* *Butterfly closure of a clean, straight wound. The advantage of this bandage is that the wound can be adequately held together and heal without a suture.*

HOW TO FEEL A PULSE

The most convenient location for feeling a pulse is over the artery of the wrist. The artery is located on the thumb side of the wrist. Use the tips of the index finger and the middle finger. Only gentle pressure is required. Locate the artery by feeling just above the base of the thumb, in the wrist. *See Figure 7.*

FIG. 7 *FEELING A PULSE AT THE WRIST* Use tips of *index finger and long (middle) finger. The pulse can be felt at the wrist just above the base of the thumb. If you can't seem to feel the pulse, move your fingers around ever so slightly and soon you'll get the right spot. (Black line indicates location of the wrist pulse.)*

Once the first-aider is certain that he is feeling the rhythmic beat of the pulse, he should count the number of beats per minute. The average adult, at rest, has about 72 pulsations per minute. Infants and children have a slightly faster rate (120 in newborns, becoming gradually slower as the child gets older).

After counting a pulse, it is wise to record it for future reference and not to rely on memory.

If the wrist pulse is not easily found, the first-aider should shift the position of his fingers slightly and increase or decrease the pressure. If the pulse is still not felt, try the other wrist. The pulse may be more easily obtained on one wrist rather than the other.

If the pulse still cannot be located, try the carotid pulse in the neck. *See Figure 8*.

First locate the "Adam's apple" with the index finger and long (middle) finger. Slide the fingers over to the side of the windpipe and feel deep into the neck. A pulse beat may be located in the carotid when it cannot be felt at the wrist.

Another available pulse is that of the femoral artery, located deep in the groin. *Figure 13 on page 50* shows a first-aider pressing on the femoral artery to control excessive bleeding in the lower extremity. Far less forceful pressure in the same spot will reveal the pulsation.

NOTE: Be certain that what you are feeling is the victim's pulse beat and not your own. If you are uncertain, feel your own pulse, and then check that of the victim. There should be a difference in quality and rate.

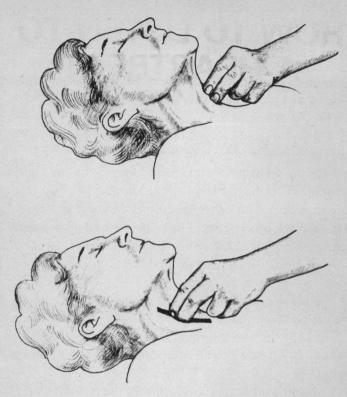

FIG. 8 FEELING A PULSE IN THE NECK *Locate the "Adam's apple" with the index finger and long (middle) finger. Then slide the fingers to the side of the windpipe, and feel the pulse deep in the neck. Black line indicates location of the carotid artery.*

HOW TO LISTEN TO A HEARTBEAT

The heart lies in the middle of the chest, beween the right lung and the left lung. *See Figure 9.* The heart extends slightly towards the left. The left ventricle can be felt and can be heard as it pulsates. The exact position where a

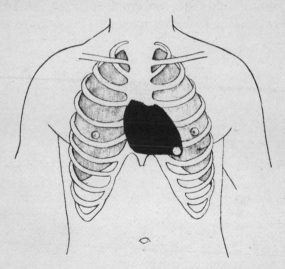

FIG. 9 *CHEST AND LOCATION OF HEART* *The heart lies between the lungs. The lungs appear here in gray, and the heart in black. A white spot shown on the black surface indicates the precise point at which the first-aider will best hear the victim's heart.*

first-aider should listen to the heartbeat is slightly below and to the left of the left nipple in a man or child.

In a mature female patient, the position of the left nipple is quite variable and is not a good guide. Raise the left breast up toward the victim's head. Place your ear just below the breast, and a little to the left side. *See Figure 10.* Once the heartbeat is located, use your watch or a clock and count the beats per minute.

The normal heart rate is 72 beats per minute for an adult, and is slightly faster for a child. A newborn infant has a heartbeat of 120 per minute. A heartbeat of over 100 in an adult should cause concern. Conversely, a heartbeat of less than 60 a minute is likewise a cause for concern.

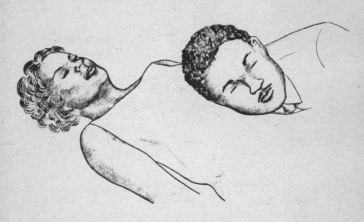

FIG. 10 *LISTENING TO A HEARTBEAT* In listening to the heartbeat of a male or a child, place the ear below the left nipple, and just to the left of the left nipple. In listening to the heartbeat of a mature female, place ear just below the left breast (not the nipple).

HOW TO CONTROL BLEEDING

TREATMENT

1. Apply a sterile dressing to the wound large enough to cover the bleeding area.

2. Apply pressure with the palm of the hand on the back of the sterile dressing. *See Figure 11.*

3. Place a bandage over the gauze dressing. Bandage firmly. *See text on page 58* on BANDAGING.

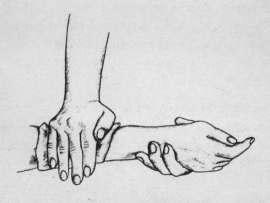

FIG. 11 *PRESSURE APPLIED ON STERILE DRESSING WITH PALM OF HAND*

If the gauze gets completely soaked with blood

Add more gauze. Do not change the dressing entirely.

If blood continues to ooze from the dressing

Apply more gauze on top of the bandage, and bandage the second dressing on top of the first dressing.

If the bleeding from an upper or lower extremity cannot be stemmed by a gauze bandage

Apply firm pressure to the artery. *See Figure 12 and Figure 13.* Hold for ten minutes and release slowly. The bleeding should then be controlled.

If the bleeding comes from the arm

The first-aider should firmly grasp the arm below the armpit, using his four fingers to tightly compress the artery. *See Figure 12.*

If the bleeding proceeds from a lower extremity

The first-aider should make a tight fist and press his fist into the artery at the groin, applying as much pressure as he can. *See Figure 13.*

If the victim's bleeding cannot be controlled by bandaging or pressure

Apply a tourniquet. *See page 51 and accompanying figures.*

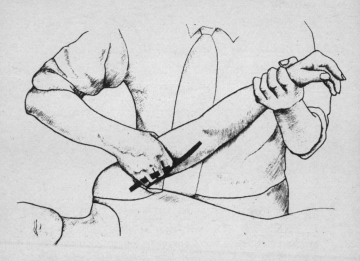

FIG. 12 *FIRST-AIDER APPLYING PRESSURE TO ARTERY OF UPPER EXTREMITY TO STEM BLEEDING The first-aider is attempting to stem excessive bleeding. The black line indicates position of artery in the upper arm. The first-aider grasps the wrist of the victim with one hand, and with his other forces his fingers into the area of the artery to exert the utmost pressure of which he is capable.*

If the victim has sustained an open fracture
See text and accompanying figures on page 236.

If the victim is suffering from shock
See page 334.

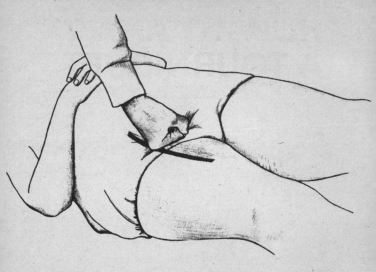

FIG. 13 *PRESSURE ON ARTERY OF LOWER EXTREMITY* *The first-aider is attempting to stop excessive bleeding. The black line represents the position of the artery in the groin. The first-aider forms a fist, and with it presses down into the artery, exerting as much pressure as he is capable of.*

What the Doctor Says Firm pressure is the best way to control most bleeding wounds. It is better to first apply a tight bandage. Then, if the bandage is too tight, it can be gently replaced later on with a looser bandage. However, if the bleeding has been fully controlled, the entire bandage can be removed and replaced with a newer dressing and a looser bandage.

HOW TO APPLY A TOURNIQUET

In applying a tourniquet, two techniques are used

1. Using an arterial tourniquet, apply enough strong pressure to stop the severe bleeding.

2. Using a venous tourniquet, apply weaker pressure, just enough to obstruct return of the blood through the veins. This tourniquet will control the toxic effects of snake or insect bites into an extremity or the effects of the injection of a medicine to which an individual is allergic.

CAUTION

- A tourniquet should *not* be used for venous bleeding, which can generally be controlled by a pressure dressing alone.

Material required

1. Broad, strong cloth, leather, or rubber, ½" to 1" (1 to 2 centimeters) in width. Rope or wire can be used if nothing else is available, but these materials are to be avoided, if possible.

2. For twisting the arterial tourniquet, use a piece of

wood, or some object of metal or plastic measuring approximately 6″ in length (15 cms.).

Method for controlling arterial bleeding

1. The tourniquet should be placed between the bleeding wound and the heart.

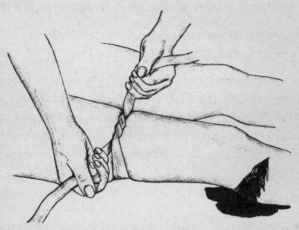

FIG. 14 *APPLYING A TOURNIQUET Place a rope around the extremity. Make two turns with the rope and pull tightly.*

2. Place cloth (or rubber tubing or belt) around the extremity. Make two turns of one end of the rope, *see Figure 14*, and pull tightly.

3. Place a strong piece of wood (cross stick), six inches (15 centimeters) long, over the turns and between the two loose ends. Tie a firm knot over the wood. *See Figure 15.*

4. To tighten the tourniquet around the extremity, pull on the wood and twist. *See Figure 16.*

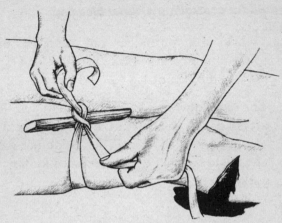

FIG. 15 *INTRODUCING THE CROSS STICK*
Place a strong piece of wood (or other suitable object) over the turns between the two loose ends, and tie a square knot firmly over the wood.

5. Keep twisting the wood until the tourniquet is sufficiently tight to stop the bleeding. Note how the tourniquet compresses the soft tissues. *See Figure 17.*

6. When the bleeding has been controlled, note the exact time when the flow has stopped, and write the time down on a piece of paper.

Method for blocking return flow of blood through the veins in snake bite, or insect bite, or to prevent absorption of injected medication. Caution: This tourniquet should not be used to control bleeding. See page 51.

1. Apply tourniquet in fashion indicated above.

2. Tighten the tourniquet only enough to cause congestion of veins—make sure that you can feel a pulse in the arm or leg.

3. The tourniquet can be kept on up to four hours, if necessary, if the victim has been bitten by a poisonous snake. In cases which do not endanger life, the tourniquet may be released for one minute out of every 15.

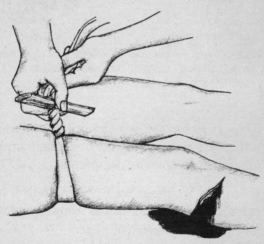

FIG. 16 *TIGHTENING THE TOURNIQUET Pull on the cross piece of wood and twist it. This will tighten the tourniquet around the extremity.*

What the Doctor Says The application of a tourniquet to a limb for control of bleeding should be reserved for severe bleeding that cannot be controlled in any other way. *See* HOW TO CONTROL BLEEDING, *page 47*. Bleeding from a torn vein can generally be controlled by direct pressure or a pressure dressing. Such wounds result in a steady flow of blood. By contrast, bleeding from an artery can be recognized by the intermittent spurt of blood at the pulse rate. It is likely that such a wound cannot be controlled by pressure alone. In severe disruptive wounds where the loss of blood is so rapid that the life of the patient may be endangered, the application of a tourniquet is a prime, life-saving measure.

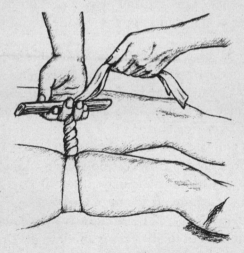

FIG. 17 *COMPLETED TOURNIQUET* *The wood has been fully tightened. Note the deep compression of the soft tissues of the thigh. At this point, the bleeding is fully controlled.*

55

To be effective, the arterial tourniquet must block the circulation completely. To allow nutrition to flow into the limb, after an hour has passed, the tourniquet should be partially untwisted and loosened for a few seconds up to one minute. If continued use is necessary, the tourniquet should be untwisted and loosened briefly every 15 minutes. The amount of bleeding that starts upon releasing the tourniquet is the guide to the duration of release. If severe bleeding promptly ensues, tighten the tourniquet immediately; it is necessary to save the victim's life, even if he loses a limb.

Fortunately, in many instances severed arteries will retract, and a clot will form and prevent further hemorrhaging. This explains why a portion of a limb may be severed completely, and yet the victim will not bleed to death.

Once in place, the tourniquet must either be held by the hand of the first-aider, or should be wrapped in place with a roller bandage and adhesive tape. *See Figure 18.* The urgency of transporting the victim to a hospital cannot be over-emphasized.

The normal pulse rate for an adult is 72 beats per minute. *See page 42.* However, following an injury the pulse rate may be faster and may run to 90 beats or even 120 beats per minute. If the victim has lost much blood and is getting weaker, the pulse rate may slow down to 60 per minute or even to 40. This is a serious development and indicates that the patient is in severe shock. In such a case, it is urgent that the victim be immediately brought to a hospital where he will be given a blood transfusion or some intravenous plasma will be administered.

In the case of a snake bite or insect bite, a tourniquet is used not for the purpose of controlling bleeding. It is rather used to block the return flow of blood through the veins into the body where such contaminated blood would have a toxic effect. Indeed, if a vein were ruptured, this type of tourniquet would *increase* bleeding.

The amount of pressure needed to block a vein is much less than that required to block an artery. A flat band around the limb should be no tighter than a snug wrist band. This flat band will render the blocked veins more visible. They may even bulge slightly. The first-aider may check whether the application of the tourniquet is proper by feeling for a pulse at the wrist, ankle, or groin. *See Figures 7 and 8 on pages 42 and 44.* The pulse should be palpable (able to be felt), and the color of the skin in between the blue veins should remain pink.

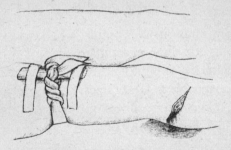

FIG. 18 *TOURNIQUET IN PLACE* *With the tourniquet held in place by strips of adhesive, bleeding is fully controlled, and the victim may be transported to a hospital.*

BANDAGING

The purpose of applying a bandage is

1. To cover an abrasion or a wound.

2. To control bleeding by means of pressure.

3. To hold some protective padding over a sensitive area.

Techniques of bandaging are varied. Only the more common methods are described here. The serious first-aider should study and practice bandaging by taking a first aid course. Such courses are given by the American National Red Cross, and by many high schools and colleges. For specific information as to where you can take a first aid course in your local district, write to the American National Red Cross, Washington, D.C. 20006.

BAND-AIDS

For simple abrasions or wounds, a band-aid is satisfactory. Band-aids come in standard sizes of ¾ of an inch (1.8 centimeters) and one-inch (2.5 centimeters). They are also obtainable in larger sizes. Some contain a gauze dressing, others a non-adherent dressing, still others are impregnated with an antiseptic.

How to apply a band-aid

1. Wash the affected area with soap and water.

2. If antibiotic ointment, such as *Neosporin, Bacimycin* or *Furacin*, is available, it would be well to put a thin layer of such ointment over the wound or on the band-aid.

3. Allow the skin to dry before applying the band-aid.

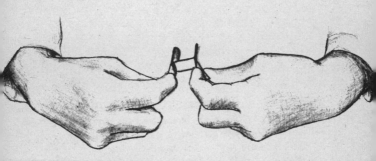

FIG. 19 *SEPARATING THE BAND-AID The first-aider grasps the two ends with his fingers, using both hands. He then gently pulls the plastic covering off the adhesive parts.*

4. Remove the paper covering on the band-aid.

5. Grasp the band-aid by its two ends with your fingers. Do not touch the sterile gauze of the center portion. *See Figure 19.*

6. Place the sterile center portion over the affected area. Now pull both tabs in opposite directions. The band-aid will now stick to the skin and is fixed firmly in place. *See Figure 20.*

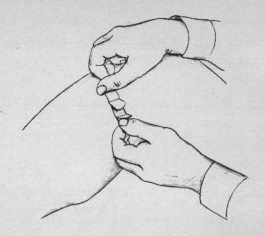

FIG. 20 *APPLYING A BAND-AID TO A WOUND The first-aider places the sterile gauze portion directly on the wound, and then pulls the band-aid in two directions so that the adhesive tabs stick to the skin.*

APPLYING A CIRCULAR BANDAGE

Circular bandaging is suitable for an injury to the wrist, or for an injury in the region just above the ankle, or for an area that does not vary much in shape, such as a finger, or the neck.

A plain gauze roller bandage may be used or one can use a non-adhesive, elastic gauze bandage. Such a bandage adheres by itself.*

*Kling by Johnson & Johnson, New Brunswick, New Jersey 08903, or Kerlex Bandage by Kendall (Bauer & Black), 80 Dean Street, Englewood, New Jersey 07631.

Technique

1. With your left thumb, hold the bandage in place on the affected part.

2. With your right hand, roll the bandage around the affected part. Make two turns over the same spot. *See Figure 21.*

3. After the first two turns, overlap each previous turn by three-quarters of its width. Always proceed in the same direction. *See Figure 22.*

4. Secure the bandage in any of the following ways:

    a. Cut the end of the bandage with scissors, and apply a piece of adhesive tape to hold bandage in place.

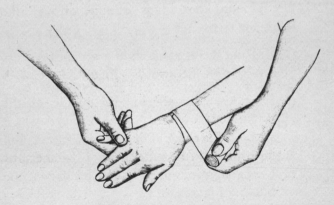

FIG. 21 *APPLYING ROLLER GAUZE BANDAGE First-aider is making simple circular turns of bandage.*

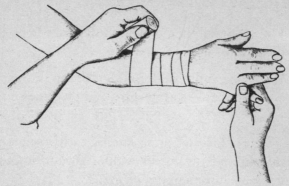

FIG. 22 *APPLYING ROLLER GAUZE BANDAGE* *First-aider overlaps each previous turn of the gauze bandage by covering three-quarters of that turn.*

b. Cut the end of the bandage with scissors, and secure the bandage with a safety pin.

c. Use a loop knot. This is done through the following steps:

(1) Roll out the bandage about eight inches in the direction of the turn. *See Figure 23.*

(2) Place two fingers in the middle of the extension. Now with the two fingers which are placed in the middle of the extension, pull the bandage in the same direction that the turns were going, forming a loop of bandage at one end. *See Figure 24.*

(3) Now, using the looped end and the plain end, make a knot. *See Figure 25.*

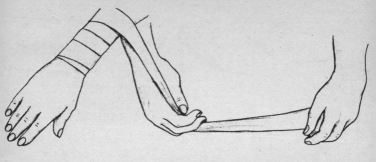

FIG. 23 KNOTTING A CIRCULAR BAN-DAGE First Step The first-aider has, at this point, rolled the gauze bandage around the affected part. He then extends the bandage eight inches (20 centimeters) out, and then places two fingers on the upper surface of the bandage.

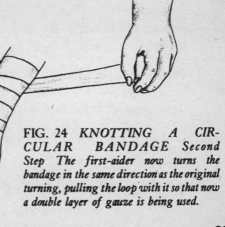

FIG. 24 KNOTTING A CIR-CULAR BANDAGE Second Step The first-aider now turns the bandage in the same direction as the original turning, pulling the loop with it so that now a double layer of gauze is being used.

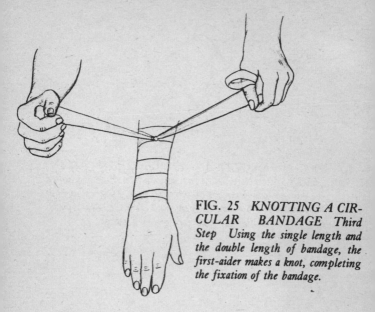

FIG. 25 KNOTTING A CIR-
CULAR BANDAGE *Third
Step Using the single length and
the double length of bandage, the
first-aider makes a knot, completing
the fixation of the bandage.*

d. Secure the bandage by dividing the bandage in
two parts. This is done in the following manner:

(1) Use scissors to cut the bandage in half. *See
Figure 26.* The bandage will now show as a
letter "V." *See Figure 27.*

(2) Form a knot with two hands. *See Figure 28.*

(3) Then tie the two ends completly around the
affected part, and secure the bandage with a
knot. *See Figure 29.*

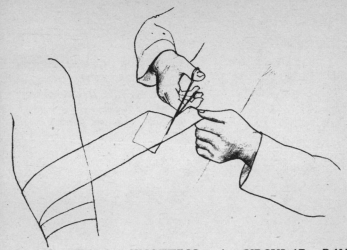

FIG. 26 *KNOTTING A CIRCULAR BAN-DAGE SECOND METHOD First Step Cut the end of the bandage about eight inches (20 centimeters) in length.*

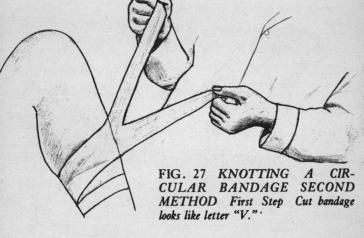

FIG. 27 *KNOTTING A CIR-CULAR BANDAGE SECOND METHOD First Step Cut bandage looks like letter "V."*

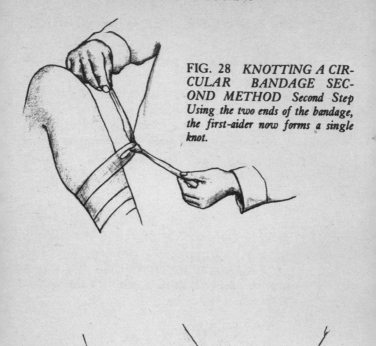

FIG. 28 KNOTTING A CIRCULAR BANDAGE SECOND METHOD *Second Step Using the two ends of the bandage, the first-aider now forms a single knot.*

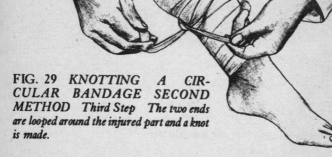

FIG. 29 KNOTTING A CIRCULAR BANDAGE SECOND METHOD *Third Step The two ends are looped around the injured part and a knot is made.*

APPLYING A SPIRAL REVERSE BANDAGE

The spiral reverse bandage is particularly suited for the thigh or for the leg.

Technique

1. With a gauze bandage, make two circular turns around the affected part. *See Figure 30.*

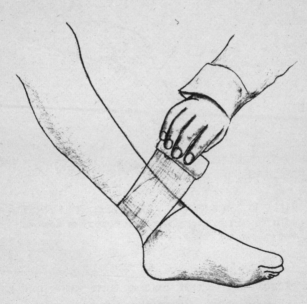

FIG. 30 *MAKING SPIRAL REVERSE TURNS First Step First-aider makes two circular turns around affected part with gauze bandage.*

67

2. Now give the bandage roll a 180 degree twist on itself, but continue bandaging in the same direction. *See Figure 31.*

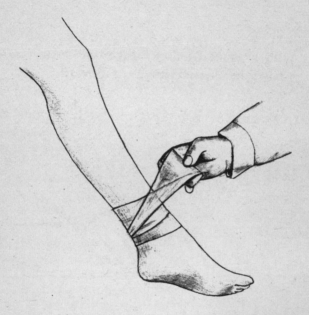

FIG. 31 *MAKING SPIRAL REVERSE TURNS Second Step Twist the bandage on itself just once and continue bandaging.*

3. Repeat this spiral reverse turn each time the bandage makes one complete circle around the part. All of the reverses should be in the same line. *See Figure 32.*

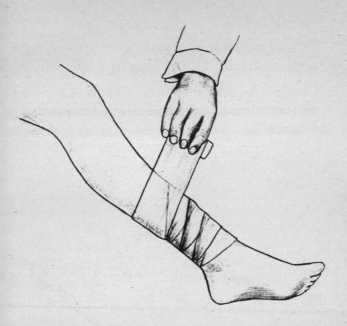

FIG. 32 *MAKING SPIRAL REVERSE TURNS* *Third Step* *Each time the first-aider comes to the point of the first twist, he twists the bandage once again. The twists should all appear to be in the same line as if the bandage were forming a design.*

APPLYING A FIGURE-OF-EIGHT BANDAGE

A figure-of-eight bandage is good for the ankle, for the knee, for the wrist and the hand, and for the elbow.

Technique

1. To start the bandage, begin by making two circular turns around the affected part. *See Figure 30.*

2. Continue by rolling the bandage obliquely across the foot, beginning the figure-of-eight pattern. *See Figure 33.*

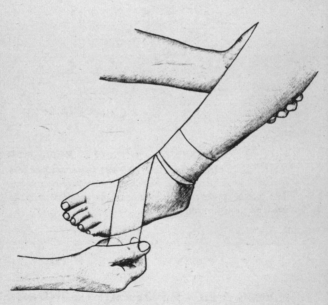

FIG. 33 *FIGURE-OF-EIGHT BANDAGE The first-aider starts by making two circular turns of the roller bandage above the ankle. He continues by rolling the bandage obliquely across the foot, beginning the figure-of-eight turn.*

3. Then make figure-of-eight turns overlapping the previous bandage on three-quarters of its width. Continue until the area is covered. *See Figure 34.*

FIG. 34 *FIGURE-OF-EIGHT BANDAGE BEING COMPLETED* *The first-aider continues by running the bandage over the foot and then under the foot and then back again around the ankle. He proceeds in this manner, back and forth, until bandaging is completed.*

APPLYING A SPICA BANDAGE

A Spica bandage is used to cover the groin or the shoulder. The Spica bandage consists of a figure-of-eight bandage, *see page 69*, which encircles the body as well as the limb.

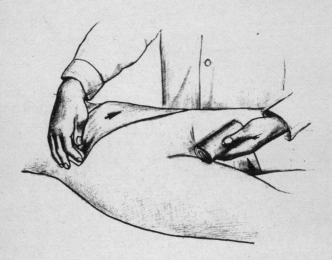

FIG. 35 *APPLYING A SPICA BANDAGE* *First & Second Steps   The first-aider is shown bandaging a hip. The victim lies flat on a table. The first-aider places the gauze bandage on top of the opposite hip, and then draws the bandage under the victim's leg.*

Technique

1. If the groin is to be bandaged, place the roller bandage on the front of the pelvis opposite the affected groin. If the shoulder is to be bandaged,

place the roller bandage in front of the opposite shoulder.

2. Then circle the affected arm or the affected leg with the bandage. *See Figure 35.*

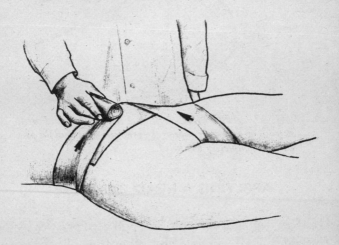

FIG. 36 *APPLYING A SPICA BANDAGE Third Step* The first-aider draws the bandage across the victim's leg, then runs the bandage underneath the small of the back of the victim, and then runs the bandage to the point where he originally started.

3. Return bandage to the pelvis. Continue by rolling the bandage behind the body. *See Figure 36.*

4. Repeat this sequence until the bandage adequately covers the affected part. *See Figure 37.*

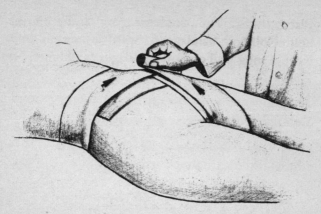

FIG. 37   *APPLYING A SPICA BANDAGE   Fourth Step   The first-aider repeats the previous turns until the part has been completely bandaged.*

APPLYING A HEAD BANDAGE

Head bandaging is difficult, and will need practice by the first-aider—more so than any other type of bandaging.

Technique

1. Use two bandages whose ends are tied together. *See Figure 38.*

FIG. 38   *TWO GAUZE ROLLER BANDAGES TIED END TO END   This is done by tying a knot, joining both ends.*

2. Place the knot of the tied bandages at the back of the head. Roll both bandages forward at the same time. Keep a snug pull on both bandages at all times. *See Figure 39.*

3. The bandages will cross each other at the forehead. *See Figure 40.*

4. Now simultaneously roll both bandages back around the head to the point of beginning. *See Figure 41.*

FIG. 39 *HEAD BANDAGE* *Begin the head bandage by placing knot across back of victim's head.*

75

5. At the back of the head, loop the bandages around each other so that one bandage continues around the side of the head while the other bandage goes over the top of the head. *See Figures 41 and 42.*

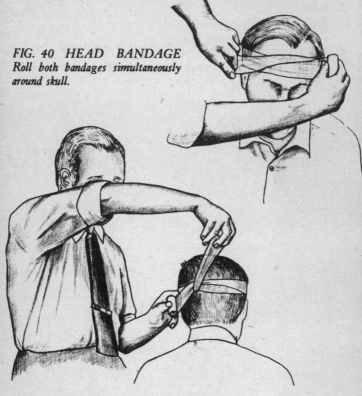

FIG. 40 *HEAD BANDAGE*
Roll both bandages simultaneously around skull.

FIG. 41 *HEAD BANDAGE Now cross one bandage back over the head, while the other bandage continues its circular turns around the forehead.*

6. On reaching the forehead, repeat the same technique used on the back of the head. *See Figure 42.*

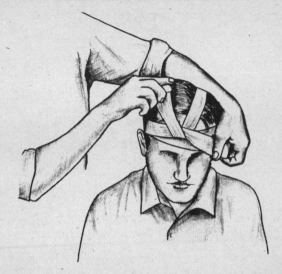

FIG. 42 *HEAD BANDAGE Now draw one bandage across top of the head, while it is being fixed in place by circular turns of the other bandage.*

7. From this point on, the bandage in one hand shuttles back and forth across the top of the head, being held in place by the bandage in the other hand. The bandage in the second hand continues to encircle the head.

8. On completing the bandage, proceed with one extra turn around the head while the shuttle bandage is held in place.

9. Then tie a knot and the bandage will be completely secured. *See Figure 43.*

FIG. 43 *HEAD BANDAGE COMPLETED After the head is completely covered, tie knot in front of forehead.*

What the Doctor Says Other techniques of bandaging may be employed successfully. For example, a bandage that sticks to itself, such as a Kurlex or a Kling, will stay in place much better than the ordinary gauze roller bandage.

Another type of bandage that may be used is the elastic bandage, which not only provides continuous pressure to control bleeding and swelling, but also furnishes slightly more in the way of immobilization. Of course, an elastic bandage will not afford as much support as a splint, but it can be helpful in treating a bleeding wound or an injury to an ankle.

If no bandaging material is available, the first-aider must improvise. If possible, he should tear a clean piece of cloth—such as a sheet, a pillowcase, or a towel—into usable strips for bandaging or splinting.

HOW TO MAKE A SPLINT

Material required

1. Rigid splinting material, such as a piece of wood, a piece of metal, or a piece of strong cardboard. *See Figure 44.*

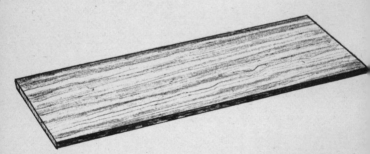

FIG. 44 *BOARD USED FOR SPLINT* The size of the board is determined by the size of the part to be splinted.

2. Strong padding material, such as a roll of absorbent cotton, a piece of cloth, a piece of felt, or a piece of sponge rubber.

3. A roller bandage two, three, or four inches wide. *See Figure 2, number 8, on page 33.*

Technique

1. Cut an adequate length of rigid material, long enough to apply to the length of the forearm or the length of the leg you expect to render rigid. If no rigid material is available, the first-aider can fold up a newspaper or magazine and use it as a splint for the forearm. This type of splint can also be used in an emergency for a broken leg. *See Figure 45.*

FIG. 45 *SPLINTING A FOREARM The first-aider is using a folded newspaper as an improvised splint.*

2. Cover one side only with soft padding material. *See Figure 46.*

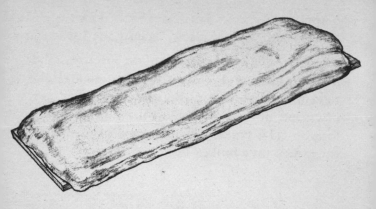

FIG. 46 *PADDING ON BOARD* This can be a piece of absorbent cotton, a piece of cloth, a piece of sponge rubber, or any piece of soft material.

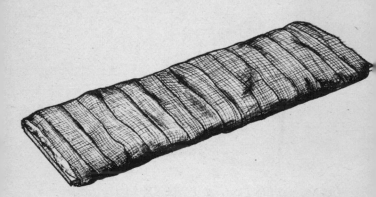

FIG. 47 *PADDED MATERIAL BANDAGED TO SPLINT BOARD*

3. Hold padding in place with a bandage. *See Figure 47.*

82

4. Apply the padded splint to the part, making sure that the padded side is placed against the broken or injured limb.

5. Tie the splint in place with a bandage, *see Figure 48,* or make single ties at intervals.

FIG. 48 *BANDAGING A SPLINT The first-aider uses a gauze roller bandage to hold splint in place.*

HOW TO MAKE A PILLOW SPLINT

Material required

1. Average-sized sleeping pillow.

2. Roller gauze bandage, or cord, rope or string.

Technique

1. Place the leg in the center of the pillow in the direction of the pillow's greatest length.

2. Fix the pillow firmly in place, using four separate ties of roller bandage, cord, or string. *See Figure 49.*

FIG. 49 *PILLOW SPLINT TIED IN PLACE The first-aider is tying a pillow snugly in place around an injured leg. A gauze roller bandage is being used.*

HOW TO MAKE A PADDED WOODEN SPLINT

Material required

1. Three boards of adequate length.

2. Padding material, such as absorbent cotton, cloth, sponge rubber, or any soft material.

3. Roller bandage, or cord, rope or string.

Technique

1. Cut three adequate lengths of rigid material, each long enough to apply to the length of the lower extremity you expect to render rigid.

2. Arrange the three pieces of wood in the form of the letter "U" so as to form a trough in which the injured limb can be placed.

3. Insert padding material into the trough so that the leg is padded against contact with the wood.

4. Place the leg inside the padded splint.

5. Tie the splint in place with four separate bandages. *See Figure 50.*

FIG. 50 *PADDED WOODEN SPLINT TIED IN PLACE   Injured leg is encased in a padding which is protected by three boards. The wooden splint is tied in place, at intervals, with a gauze bandage.*

If no splinting material is available

Use the good leg as a brace against which to fix and fasten the injured leg. *See Figure 51.*

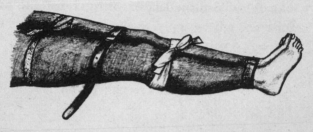

FIG. 51 *INJURED LEG TIED TO HEALTHY LEG* In the absence of splinting material, a necktie, a belt, and pieces of cloth have been used.

What the Doctor Says The purposes of splinting are to:

1. Afford some rigidity and support to the upper extremities, lower extremities, or the trunk.

2. Control pain.

3. Control bleeding.

4. Prevent further injury.

5. Permit safe transportation.

To achieve these ends, the first-aider should:

1. Pad the zone between the part and the splint. If the splinted arm is pressed against the body, also pad the area between the arm and the body.

2. Fix the splint in place with a bandage, or with strips of cloth, or with a belt, or with some improvised method.

Once these principles are understood, the first-aider has much leeway in improvising splints. He may employ whatever material is available—hay, grass, branches of trees, boards, cardboard, magazines, newspapers, laces, etc.

In general, "Splint them where they lie" is a good principle. But if the victim is in an area that is dangerous because of fire, explosion, traffic, or extreme weather conditions, it may be necessary to move the victim to a safe spot before rendering first aid.

Possible fractures or dislocations should not be set by the first-aider. Nonetheless, he may employ longitudinal traction—a firm but not too vigorous pulling force—while applying a splint to an extremity. If possible, one first-aider should apply the traction and stabilize the extremity while another first-aider applies the splint.

A trained layman can offer more sophisticated help than is indicated above by administering professional type splinting. This requires training. Courses in how to do professional splinting are given by the American National Red Cross, the American Academy of Orthopaedic Surgeons, and the American College of Surgeons. For further information, write to any of the following addresses:

American National Red Cross, Washington, D.C. 20006.

American Academy of Orthopaedic Surgeons, 430 North Michigan Avenue, Chicago, Illinois 60611.

American College of Surgeons, 55 East Erie Street, Chicago, Illinois 60611.

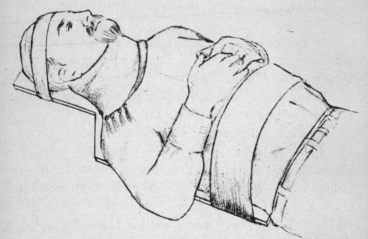

FIG. 52 *USE OF SHORT BOARD* *The victim has suffered a fracture of the neck, and has been fixed to the short board to permit transportation. Note that an improvised collar has been applied to the neck, and that both the forehead and the chest have been strapped to the board.*

APPLYING A PNEUMATIC SPLINT

A pneumatic splint called *Redisplint** is an effective method of obtaining temporary immobilization for the purpose of transporting the victim to a hospital. The pneumatic splint consists of a double-walled plastic tube placed around the affected part which is first zippered closed and then inflated by mouth. A splint of adequate firmness is instantly formed which will support a broken bone and will also control bleeding from the veins. Where there is arterial bleeding, a pneumatic splint will exert pressure on the dressings and therefore inhibit the loss of blood. A pneumatic splint is transparent and permits visual inspection of the wound; its presence does not interfere with X-ray examination.

Instructions in the use of *Redisplint* are included in the package. *See also Figures 53, 54, 55 and 56.*

Only a first-aider who has taken special training will be sufficiently skilled to use a pneumatic splint. It is worthwhile learning, for this air splint is particularly effective. It comes in various sizes for use on both the upper and lower extremities.

*Parke-Davis. Six sizes: 1. Hand and wrist. 2. Half arm. 3. Full arm. 4. Foot and ankle. 5. Half leg. 6. Full leg.

Various types of metal splints are also available. The *Thomas* splint* is particularly effective in transporting a victim whose lower extremity has been wounded.

FIG. 53 *PLACING PNEUMATIC SPLINT ON LEG*

---

*This is a metal splint which can bandage the limb. It will also apply traction to the extremity while the victim is being transported to a hospital. To apply this splint properly, a first-aider should have had special training.

FIG. 54 *ZIPPING UP PNEUMATIC SPLINT*

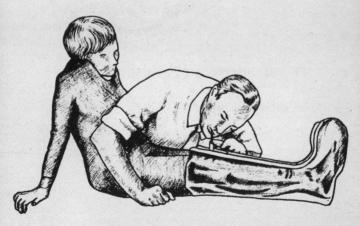

FIG. 55 *BLOWING UP PNEUMATIC SPLINT*

FIG. 56 BLOWN-UP PNEUMATIC SPLINT

HOW TO MAKE A SLING

Technique

1. Use any piece of cloth. A sheet, a large towel, or a blanket will do fine.

2. Cut the cloth into the shape of a triangle approximately 3 feet x 3 feet x 4 feet (90 x 90 x 120 cm.).

FIG. 57 *APPLYING SLING   First-aider places triangular bandage underneath injured arm.*

3. Hold one end of the triangular piece of cloth in back of the victim's neck.

4. Now draw the cloth down so that the elbow rests inside of the wide part of the cloth. *See Figure 57.*

5. Tie a knot behind the neck. The elbow will now be supported securely inside the sling. *See Figure 58.*

FIG. 58 *COMPLETED SLING TIED AROUND BACK OF NECK*

If no scissors are available

Tear the cloth into the same shape and size.

If no cloth is available

Then use a belt for a sling. *See Figure 60.*

FIG. 59 *SLING BOUND TO BODY WITH ADDITIONAL CRAVAT* This additional cravat, a Velpean-type bandage, is used to immobilize a fracture of the shoulder and upper arm.

FIG. 60   *BELT USED AS IMPROVISED SLING*

What the Doctor Says   The purpose of a sling is to support an arm, a hand, or a shoulder in order to relieve the pain which might be caused by movement. A sling, of course, overcomes the force of gravity and counteracts the normal downward pull that would otherwise be exerted.

In some situations, a sling may in itself be the most effective treatment. This would be so in cases of sprains, or minor fractures of the shoulder or elbow where there are no displaced bones.

In other instances the sling will serve as a temporary first aid measure, supporting the injured part until examination and X-ray by a physician.

Where a large piece of cloth is not available, the first-aider can use his ingenuity to tie two or three pieces of cloth together. Even a number of small handkerchiefs knotted together can make a serviceable sling. The fact is that any method of suspending the wrist from the neck will prove to be of value.

CRUTCHES

Whenever a victim suffers a fracture of the lower extremities, it is always best to have him do whatever little walking he must do by being supported on crutches. Of course, crutches are not always available. Yet, though crutches may not be present in your home, they may be present in the home of a neighbor. Let us say you live in an apartment building where somebody has been injured

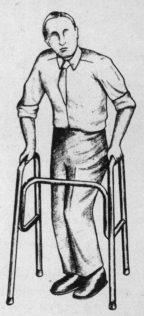

FIG. 61 *WALKER Victim grasps both sides of aluminum apparatus to afford him support and relieve weight bearing.*

and has used crutches, then by all means ask to borrow these crutches to take care of your emergency.

The use of crutches is the most effective means of taking the weight off the feet when the patient is in locomotion. A walker, if available, is another excellent method of relieving weight from the injured extremity. *See Figure 61.*

FIG. 62 SUPPORTING VICTIM *To relieve weight-bearing pressure when neither crutches nor a walker are available, first-aiders hold victim by placing their hands under his armpits.*

CARDIOPULMONARY RESUSCITATION (CPR)*

Definition   Cardiopulmonary resuscitation (CPR) consists of mouth-to-mouth resuscitation plus external cardiac massage—either or both, as the situation requires.

CAUTION

- First-aiders require training and study to apply CPR properly. Mouth-to-mouth resuscitation is a simple and safe technique of artificial respiration. External cardiac massage requires training.

CPR should be administered in the following situations:

1. Sudden heart attack. *See p. 289.*

2. Drowning. *See p. 188.*

---

*This material has been extracted from "Standards for Cardio-pulmonary Resuscitation (CPR) and Emergency Cardiac Care (ECC)," *Journal of the American Medical Association,* February 18, 1974, Vol. 227, No. 7 (Supplement). National Conference held in May 1973.

3. Asphyxiation. *See p. 307.*

4. Drug poisoning resulting from an overdose of such substances as barbiturate, sedatives, tranquilizers, heroin, or other narcotics. *See p. 191.*

5. Electrocution. *See p. 196.*

6. Suffocation.

7. Cessation of breathing due to the concussion of an explosion.

8. Partial obstruction of breathing because of the presence of a foreign object in the air passages. *See p. 231.*

9. A severe automobile accident in which the victim has lost consciousness and may be dying.

There must be a maximum sense of urgency before starting heart massage. CPR must be initiated within four minutes after the victim has been stricken. There is no time to transport the victim to a hospital.

A rapid determination by the first-aider of two findings must be made before beginning CPR:

One, that the victim is not breathing, as indicated by either little or no movement of the chest or upper abdomen, and by no movement of air through the nose or mouth.

Two, that the heart is not pumping: no pulse is felt in the large arteries of the neck or the groin. *See Figure 8, page 44.* No heartbeat is detected. *See Figure 10, page 46.*

TREATMENT

1. *If the victim is not breathing but the heart is still pumping,* only mouth-to-mouth breathing is needed.

2. *If the heart is not pumping,* external cardiac massage is also required, in addition to artificial respiration. Artificial respiration is always required when external cardiac compression is used. Give four rapid mouth-to-mouth breaths before proceeding with CPR.

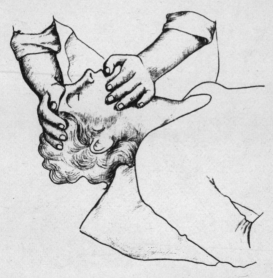

FIG. 63 *MOUTH-TO-MOUTH BREATHING Place a pillow under the victim's shoulder. To clear passages to lungs, bend the victim's head back as far as it will go.*

How to administer mouth-to-mouth breathing

1. If you suspect there is foreign matter in the victim's mouth, such as seaweed in the case of drowning, then clean out the victim's mouth with your index finger. *See Figure 112 on page 233.*

2. Place pillow under victim's shoulder. *See Figure 63.*

3. To clear passages to lungs, bend the victim's head back as far as it will go. *See Figure 63.*

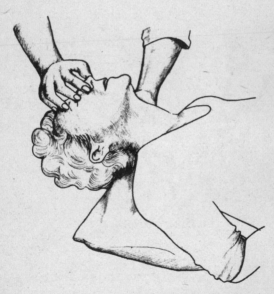

FIG. 64 *MOUTH-TO-MOUTH BREATHING* *Place one hand in back of victim's neck, and then pinch off the nostrils with the other.*

4. Place one hand in back of victim's neck. *See Figure 64.*

5. Pinch off victim's nostrils with other hand. *See Figure 64.*

6. Seal your lips around victim's open mouth to shut off loss of air. *See Figure 65.*

FIG. 65 *MOUTH-TO-MOUTH BREATHING Seal your lips around victim's mouth to shut off loss of air. Blow air forcibly into victim's open mouth.*

103

7. Blow air forcibly into victim's open mouth. *See Figure 65.*

8. Remove your mouth from victim's mouth. This will enable you to inhale, and will also permit air to exhale from victim's mouth.

9. Repeat this process until victim is able to breathe. Maintain a regular rhythm of inhaling and exhaling—12 to 15 per minute—for up to four hours.

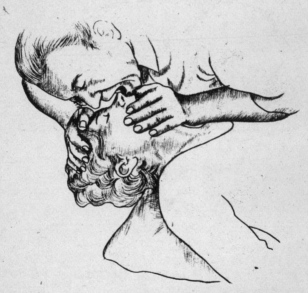

FIG. 66 *MOUTH-TO-NOSE BREATHING Place your right hand on victim's forehead. Now seal victim's mouth with other hand. Place your lips around victim's nose.*

How to administer mouth-to-nose breathing

1. Place pillow under victim's shoulder. *See Figure 63.*

2. To clear passages to lungs, bend the victim's head back as far as it will go. *See Figure 63.*

3. Place one hand on victim's forehead. *See Figure 66.*

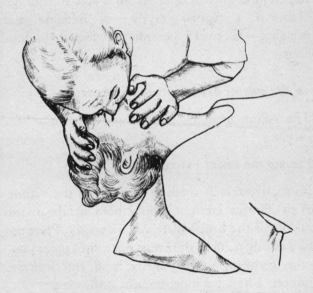

FIG. 67 *MOUTH-TO-NOSE BREATHING With lips tightly sealed around victim's nose, blow air forcibly into nostrils.*

4. Seal victim's mouth with other hand. *See Figure 66.*

105

5. Place your lips tightly around victim's nose. *See Figure 66*.

6. Blow air forcibly into victim's nostrils. *See Figure 67*.

7. Remove your lips from victim's nose. This will enable you to inhale, and will also permit air to exhale from victim's nose.

8. Repeat this process until victim is able to breathe. Maintain a regular rhythm of inhaling and exhaling—12 to 15 per minute—for up to four hours.

How to administer external cardiac massage

1. The victim must be placed lying flat on a firm surface.

2. Elevate the lower extremities.

3. Position yourself close to one side of the victim. With elbows straight, apply both hands to the middle of the breast plate. *See Figure 68*. Place the heel of one palm to the breast plate; then place your other hand on top of the first hand. Interlock the fingers. The arms must be held stiff.

4. With shoulders directly over the breast plate, exert enough pressure straight downward to depress the breast plate at least one and a half to two inches (2.5 to 3 cms.).

5. The rate of compressions is 80 per minute. Time in seconds can be estimated satisfactorily if the rescuer thinks slowly: "a million and one, a million and two," etc. Each phrase approximates one second.

6. If two first-aiders are available, they should position themselves on opposite sides of the victim, one performing external cardiac massage, the other administering mouth-to-mouth resuscitation. The ratio of cardiac compression to mouth-to-mouth resuscitation is: five compressions followed by one mouth-to-mouth breath, without interruption of the compression rhythm.

7. If fatigue sets in, the first-aiders may quickly change positions, or they may have two other rescuers relieve them, one at a time.

8. Continue for one hour. If breathing and pulse beat have not returned, resuscitation has failed.

One first-aider may apply both mouth-to-mouth breathing and external cardiac massage. This consists of two very quick lung inflations after each fifteen compressions.

Infants and children require less forceful pressure, both in breathing and in external cardiac massage.

Special training is needed to administer these techniques.

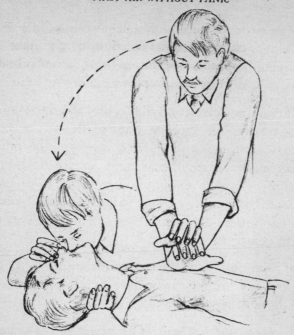

FIG. 68 *EXTERNAL CARDIAC MASSAGE (ONE RESCUER TECHNIQUE) Note that pressure is applied midway between the hollow at the upper end of the breast plate and the upper end of the pit of the stomach. The first-aider's elbow is straight, and he is pressing with the heel of his palm. The heel of his other palm is applied to the back of the bottom hand. The curved broken line indicates the shift of the rescuer to mouth-to-mouth breathing.*

How to decide if CPR is effective

1. Reaction of the pupils. *See Figure 69.* This should be checked periodically.

a. If the pupils are widely dilated and do not narrow down when a bright light is applied, this means that serious brain damage has developed.

b. If the pupils are widely dilated but react to light by narrowing down, there is still a chance the victim will survive.

2. Feel for neck pulse (carotid) after one minute of CPR and every few minutes thereafter.

FIG. 69 *SIZE OF PUPIL The eye at the top is depicted with a normal-sized pupil. The eye in the middle shows a dilated pupil. The eye at the bottom illustrates a pin-point contraction of the pupil.*

Note If after one hour of CPR the victim has not responded by spontaneous breathing and a sustained pulse, and if the pupils are widely dilated, *see Figure 69,* and do not contract down when a bright light is applied, discontinue treatment.

Pre-Cardial Thump A single sharp blow to the chest over the mid-portion of the breast plate (sternum). Hit with a closed fist, thumb upward. This requires special training. *See Figure 70.*

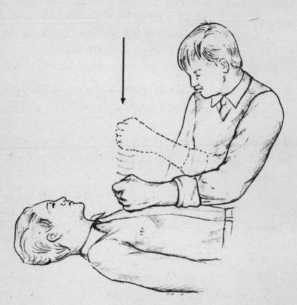

FIG. 70 *PRE-CARDIAL THUMP A single sharp blow is applied to the midpoint of the breast plate (sternum), with the (thumb up) side of the closed fist.*

CAUTION

- This treatment should be applied only if you are present when an adult suffers a heart attack. Pre-cardial thump is not to be used on children!

The thump must be delivered within the first minute after cardiac arrest.

If the victim suffers a heart attack and loses consciousness:

1. Immediately tilt the victim's head to open the airway. *See Figure 63.* At the same time, feel the neck pulse (carotid). *See Figure 8 on page 44.*

2. If no pulse is felt, administer a pre-cardial thump.

3. If the victim is not breathing, give four quick full mouth-to-mouth breaths.

4. If pulse and breathing are not immediately restored, begin one-rescuer or two-rescuer CPR.

What the Doctor Says It has been estimated that about one million persons in the United States are stricken by heart attack each year. More than 650,000 victims die. Of these deaths, about 350,000 occur outside the hospital, usually within two hours after the onset of the symptoms. An appreciable number of these deaths might have been prevented by prompt appropriate first-aid treatment.

Once you have determined the need for CPR, don't waste a second! Life or death will be determined in four to six minutes.

On the other hand, if the victim has definitely *not* been breathing for ten minutes, and if there is no pulse or heart beat, it is too late for CPR.

If the victim is suffering from terminal cancer or some other fatal disease, or has severe heart disease and heart failure, do not institute CPR.

If there is doubt about whether to start CPR or not, the reaction of the pupils to bright light may be a determining factor. If they contract, there is hope. If they remain widely dilated, then permanent brain damage has already occurred, and CPR will be futile.

It should be kept in mind that there are two things the first-aider must accomplish in CPR: (1) Clearing the airway and breathing oxygen into the lungs preparatory to (2) compression of the heart, forceful enough to drive blood through the lungs to pick up the waiting oxygen and bring that oxygen to the brain. A correct amount of force and proper coordination are necessary to accomplish both of these objectives.

If too much force is used or if pressure is applied in the wrong spot in external cardiac massage, damage may be inflicted. Pressure too high in the breast plate will not be effective. Pressure too much to the sides of the breast plate may fracture ribs. Pressure too low on the breast plate may rupture the liver or spleen. The pressure should be applied to the midpoint of the breast plate, strictly in the mid-line, and not to the side. *See Figure 68.*

To test the effectiveness of external cardiac massage, another rescuer should feel for the pulsation of blood flowing through the large vessel in the neck (carotid artery) or in the groin (femoral artery) during the application of external cardiac massage.

To test the effectiveness of mouth-to-mouth resuscitation, the rescuer should observe the heaving of the chest as blowing pressure is applied.

Signs of recovery are:

1. Return of pulse to the victim's neck or to the groin.

2. Return of breathing; at first, this may be gasping and intermittent.

3. Pupils becoming constricted from a dilated position; this is evidence that oxygen is reaching the brain.

4. Movements of the arms or legs.

5. Color of the skin improving from pale blue to light pink.

6. Return of a heart beat and a pulse beat in the neck, the groin or at the wrist.

If after one hour of CPR none of the above signs is detected, the first-aider should discontinue his efforts.

It cannot be over-emphasized that training and practice are required to develop efficiency in the above techniques. All first-aiders are urged to enroll in a course for this purpose.

Once the techniques are mastered, this section can serve as a quick review and a reminder of the correct procedures.

It should be noted that CPR is one first-aid

procedure that can be accomplished without equipment. A willing and interested person, as young as 13 or 14, can be trained to perform cardiopulmonary resuscitation successfully.

More advanced first-aiders—Emergency Medical Technicians, for example—may use equipment such as plastic airways in conjunction with oxygen tanks and bags that force oxygen into the lungs.

A physician treating a victim might insert a tube in the windpipe (trachea) to keep the airway completely open.

There are also mechanical devices for applying external cardiac massage. In a hospital, a physician may deem it necessary to apply an electrical current to the heart with an apparatus known as a defibrillator. This would be used if the cause of a cardiac arrest were ventricular fibrillation, a very rapid, irregular, and weak heartbeat.

TRACHEOSTOMY

(Surgical Opening into the Windpipe)

When to perform an emergency (stab) tracheostomy

This heroic procedure should be applied *only if the victim is suffocating from an obstruction of breathing and when every second of time is important.* The obstruction might be caused by a foreign body, such as a piece of meat, blocking the voice box (larynx), or by an acute swelling of the larynx due to an injury, or some inflammation, or because of burns. *See pages 146, 156, and 231.* An individual who has swallowed a piece of meat may appear to be suffering from a heart attack. The key to diagnosis is that the person with a blocked larynx will be unable to say a word, while an individual with an acute heart attack will be able to speak, even if only in a weak voice. If the windpipe is blocked, emergency treatment is likely necessary to avoid suffocation and death. Speed is essential.

Technique of stab tracheostomy

1. Lie the victim flat on the ground or on a bed or on a couch, with a pillow or any equivalent object behind

the shoulder blades of the victim. (Do not waste time finding a pillow if it is not readily available.)

2. Push the chin back sufficiently to make the Adam's apple, *see Figure 71*, stand out prominently, and to render the front of the neck somewhat taut.

3. Feel for a depression in the midline of the neck, about one inch (2.5 cms.) below the top of the Adam's apple. *See Figure 71*.

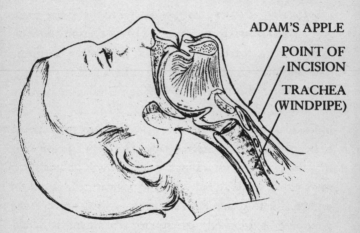

ADAM'S APPLE

POINT OF INCISION

TRACHEA (WINDPIPE)

FIG. 71 *TRACHEOSTOMY*

4. Hold the windpipe at the level of this depression on both sides with the index finger and thumb.

5. Make an incision one inch (2.5 cms.) long longitudinally, staying strictly in the midline. *See Figure 72*.

6. Little bleeding will be encountered. Continue the incision through the entire depth of the skin until fatty tissue appears. Fatty tissue looks yellow. Deep into that tissue, a whitish firm membrane (cricothyroid) will be encountered.

7. Make a transverse cut (horizontal or vertical) through this membrane, one half inch (2 cm.) into the windpipe. Be sure that air can pass through the opening.

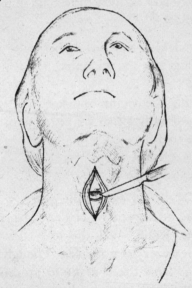

FIG. 72 *STAB TRACHEOSTOMY*
Note that the longitudinal incision has penetrated through the skin, the underlying fat, and the whitish firm membrane. The transverse incision is made directly into the trachea (windpipe).

8. To allow air to pass freely, maintain the opening by means of one of the following techniques. *See Figure 72.*

   a. Force the empty barrel of a ball-point pen through the opening into the windpipe.

   b. Force a drinking straw into the windpipe.

   c. Hold the opening apart by using, for instance, a knife on one side and a key on the other side, or employ any equivalent technique to separate the tissues.

   d. If available, force a rubber tube through the opening into the windpipe.

9. Stay with the victim and keep the tracheostomy open until a physician arrives or until the victim is brought to a hospital.

What the Doctor Says Emergency tracheostomy should not be attempted by a first-aider unless he is convinced the victim will die in a few minutes if emergency measures are not taken. Though many first-aiders will not have the courage to proceed with this operation, the technique outlined is safe because there are no major blood vessels or nerves in the area between the skin and the hollow center of the windpipe.

There are four structures to be penetrated: (1) skin,

(2) fatty tissue under the skin, (3) the whitish firm membrane, and (4) the front of the windpipe.

If the obstruction is deep in the chest, below the larynx, then the tracheostomy will, of course, not be effective.

Similarly, if the lining membrane of the lungs is seriously blistered by the heat of fire, the tracheostomy will be of no aid.

Nevertheless, in all instances where choking is involved and the victim faces imminent death, emergency tracheostomy is justified.

EMERGENCIES

ABDOMINAL PAIN

Ordinary stomach upsets and bellyaches do not require the assistance of a first-aider. This section deals only with *severe* abdominal pain—not with every little stomach ache, food sensitivity, dietary indiscretion, or bellyache. If the first-aider is in doubt, he should contact a physician by telephone, and seek his advice as to what course to follow.

Symptoms Pain and nausea in the upper part of the abdomen, which may later shift to the right lower part of the abdomen.

CAUTION

- Give no cathartics (laxatives).

- Do not give an enema.

- Do not place ice bag on abdomen.

- Do not give the victim any food nor drink nor alcohol.

TREATMENT

Call a doctor or an ambulance immediately. Medical assistance is necessary without delay to determine the cause of the upset. The condition may be acute appendicitis, and immediate and quick attention may be necessary to save the victim's life.

What the Doctor Says The big fear in the case of strong abdominal pains is that the patient is suffering from acute appendicitis. If diarrhea is present, it is probable that the victim does not have acute appendicitis.

Pressure over the right lower abdomen will disclose a rigid muscle. This muscle may at times be as rigid as a board. If the first-aider finds this condition, peritoneal irritation is present.

Another test is to place the tips of the fingers on the abdomen, to press deeply and then suddenly release the pressure. Acute pain reaction ("rebound tenderness") indicates that there is a peritoneal irritation. The intestinal tract may be perforated by an ulceration; the gall bladder may be inflamed; or acute appendicitis may be present. A rigid abdomen and rebound tenderness are signs of a serious condition and no time should be lost in rushing the victim to a hospital.

However, a severe case of diarrhea may also cause abdominal pain and colic, and require medical attention.

Excruciating abdominal pain may be caused by the presence of a kidney stone (renal colic). Pain will be experienced in the flank and/or the groin. First aid consists of some form of sedation for severe pain pending medical assistance.

Gallstones may cause acute abdominal pain. In all these situations, the first-aider should not apply either hot or cold applications to the abdomen since these may either aggravate or mask the symptoms. Keep the victim lying still on his back until medical aid can be obtained. The victim should not walk, but should be carried to the hospital. Walking may be dangerous because it may aggravate the trouble in the abdomen, and because the patient may faint and fall to the ground, causing injury.

For further discussion, *see* DIARRHEA on *page 186,* and FOOD POISONING on *page 220*.

AMPUTATION

Definition   The total loss of a part of the body, such as a finger tip, a hand, an arm, a foot or an ear, through an injury.

CAUTION

- Do not put the severed part in alcohol or in water or in any fluid.

- Do not give the victim food or water.

- Have the victim lie down.

- If the patient has fainted, or is in shock, follow instructions on *page 334* for treatment of shock.

TREATMENT

1. Treat the severed end of the body as indicated on *page 364* for treatment of wounds. *See page 47* for control of bleeding. If necessary, follow instructions for treatment of shock on *page 334*.

2. Immediately summon a physician or an ambulance.

3. Place the severed part in a clean piece of cloth, or in a clean or sterile bottle, and keep it for the doctor.

4. If possible, alert the hospital or doctor in advance of your forthcoming arrival with a victim of amputation due to injury.

FIG. 73 *AMPUTATED TIPS OF THREE FINGERS Victim's hand was caught in a meat slicer.*

What the Doctor Says   Accidents involving amputation are usually caused by the victim himself cutting off a finger with a knife or a cleaver, during kitchen work. Frequently, they are caused when a part of the body has been caught in a machine in a factory, or chopped off with an axe. Railroad or automobile accidents are occasionally responsible.

Amputations sometimes occur in a brawl or a fight where one of the parties wields a knife, a sword, or a razor. In machete fights, for example, a victim may have his hand cleanly and completely amputated at the wrist.

Since modern surgery can sometimes accomplish the re-attachment of a part to the body of a victim, it is

127

imperative that the severed part be saved. If possible, the severed part should be kept cool. A small part, like the severed end of a finger, *see Figure 73,* can be re-attached by surgery, particularly if the amputation was made cleanly and did not leave too much of a jagged surface. There are case reports of larger segments of the upper or lower extremities, hands, feet, or an entire limb that were successfully re-attached.

The question may be considered as to why a victim does not bleed to death when he experiences a traumatic amputation, because it necessarily cuts completely through a large artery. Three things happen that spare a victim such profuse bleeding that would ordinarily cause death:

1. The blood vessels promptly develop a severe spasm.

2. The blood pressure becomes low.

3. The two conditions stated above foster rapid blood clot formation, sealing the blood vessels still further.

ANKLE SPRAIN

Definition An injury to the ankle joints caused by undue stretching of the ligaments.

Symptoms Severe pain and swelling of ankle following any injury. The victim generally will limp and complain of pain, and may be unable to step on the affected foot.

CAUTION

- Victim should not carry weight on his foot.

TREATMENT

1. Have the victim lie down.

2. Elevate the ankle on a pillow.

3. Apply cold in the form of an ice bag, or a cloth which has been dipped in ice water and then squeezed out. *See page 149* under WHAT THE DOCTOR SAYS.

4. Take victim to a doctor for X-ray examination. For method of transporting to a doctor, *see page 97.*

5. If medical care is not available, apply elastic bandage. *See page 35.* For method of application, see FIGURE-OF-EIGHT BANDAGE on *page 69.*

What the Doctor Says The most common cause of a

sprained ankle is a twisting or turning of the ankle in an unaccustomed manner. Occasionally, a vein will be ruptured and rapid swelling may develop in a matter of minutes. When an ankle is injured, a doctor must determine whether a fracture was sustained or whether only a ligament was strained. Both conditions may be equally painful. The fact is that pain in a very severe sprain may, at times, be even more severe than the pain caused by a fracture.

Until the victim has been examined by a physician and an X-ray has been obtained, the wisest course is to avoid weight bearing. In most instances, a sprained ankle will respond to the application of cold, elevation of the part, adhesive strapping, and some form of external support. Such support may be gained through crutches or by use of a cane. *See page 97.* After the ankle and foot are wrapped in some type of supporting bandage, the swelling may increase and the bandage may feel overly tight, and the victim experience an increased pain. If this occurs, the bandage should be entirely removed and the foot should be elevated, and ice applied to the affected part. A very severe sprain may require a plaster cast. Depending on the severity of the injury, two to six weeks of active treatment will be required. Some pain or swelling may persist for weeks or even months.

Sometimes a ligament of the ankle is so completely torn or ruptured that it can only be mended through operative correction and cast application. Only a qualified surgeon can make that decision.

ASTHMA

Definition   A condition where both breathing in and breathing out are difficult. This difficulty in breathing is accompanied by characteristic wheezing, due to partial obstruction of the air which results from a spasm of the breathing tubes.

TREATMENT

1. The first-aider should confidently reassure the victim that he will survive the attack.

2. If possible, move the victim away from dust, dogs, cats, smoke, fire, fumes, pollen or any contamination by particles that may irritate the lungs and aggravate the attack.

3. If the victim is on a regimen prescribed by a physician, such as a special spray for the lungs, the first-aider should follow the instructions prescribed with the medication.

4. If the victim is not responding to treatment or is getting worse—particularly if he is turning blue— seek medical attention at once.

What the Doctor Says   Asthma is commonly caused by an allergy to food or some contaminant in the air.

Psychological makeup is also a factor. Once the causes are recognized, the irritants should be avoided. If dust or pollen disturb the victim, he must either avoid the offending substance, or be desensitized through injection.

If an acute attack is unremitting, adrenalin may have to be injected by such members of the victim's family who have been fully trained in the technique.

Reassurance of the victim is especially helpful first aid.

AUTOMOBILE ACCIDENTS

Consult the section of this book that applies to the particular injuries *(see below)*.

What the Doctor Says As the years go by, automobile accidents claim more and more victims and account for an increasing number of deaths. One of the more frequent results of a collision is an injury to the head—concussion, brain hemorrhage, or brain laceration. *See page 287.* Also common are fractures, dislocations, tissue lacerations, *see page 236,* and whiplash, *see page 362.*

The use of seat belts has significantly reduced such injuries, but seat belts do not prevent strains of the neck, back, and extremities. Moreover, tearing out of the seat belt attachment may expose the passenger to serious injuries.

If an accident occurs on a highway where traffic is flowing, the first-aider should promptly halt or divert traffic, or if possible, move the vehicle and the victim to a safe location. If it is nighttime, flares should be set up. First-aiders have been killed or severely injured because they failed to follow the above rules before initiating care.

A copy of this book and a first-aid kit should be carried in every vehicle.

BACK PAIN (ACUTE)

Severe pain in the lower back may follow a strain caused by heavy lifting, or such pain may appear spontaneously.

TREATMENT

1. Have the victim lie flat on a firm surface such as the floor.

2. Gently bend both knees and hips as far as the victim permits without undue pain.

3. Reassure victim that the condition is temporary.

4. If available, administer some sedative, aspirin product, tranquilizer, sleeping pill, or pain reliever.

5. If the victim can move, advise him to go home and rest.

6. If the acute pain continues, the victim should seek medical assistance.

BITES OF ANIMALS AND HUMANS

TREATMENT

1. Wash the wound thoroughly with soap and water.

2. Rinse the wound thoroughly with hydrogen peroxide, or with an antiseptic soap, or clear running water.

3. Cover the wound with an antibiotic ointment, such as *Neosporin, Bacimycin,* or *Furacin.*

4. Bandage with a sterile dressing. *See page 364.*

If the bite is from a dog

1. Call your local Health Department immediately for instructions.

2. Keep the dog under observation. Do NOT kill the dog.

3. If the animal has been killed for one reason or another, bring the body to the Health Department for study.

If the bite is from a bird

Call the Health Department immediately.

What the Doctor Says   A bite of any type causes a scratching, penetrating or lacerated wound. The potential danger is greater than an ordinary injury because the danger of infection is greater and more serious. All bites should be treated by a physician.

Human bites are quite dangerous. Increased pain, redness, swelling, fever, and lethargy are signs of developing trouble. The mouth of a human is filled with a variety of germs which could cause serious infection.

A dog bite could cause rabies. It is extremely important to keep the dog caged and under observation. The local Health Department will advise concerning the necessity of rabies vaccine injections for the victim.

Bird contacts and bites may cause a disease called psiticosis.

The intestines of horses, dogs and other animals contain tetanus bacillus, making the possibility of tetanus infection ("lockjaw") a serious possibility. Tetanus toxoid or antitoxin injection is necessary.

Fish bites or injuries may cause serious wounds and even injected poisons. The first-aider should treat the wound as indicated in text on *page 364* dealing with the treatment of wounds. Be certain to arrange for the promptest care by a physician. *Whereas lacerations of ordinary injuries may be sutured initially, the wounds of bites should be cleansed and left open.* Delayed closure of some wounds may be desirable, but this is a decision to be made by the treating physician.

BITES OF
MARINE ANIMALS

Sharks, barracuda, moray eels, and killer whales are included in this group which includes a great number of fish.

TREATMENT

1. Control the bleeding. *See text on page 47 and accompanying figures.*

2. See treatment for WOUNDS AND LACERATIONS on page 364.

If the wound is very severe and a large segment of flesh has been ripped away

1. Stuff gauze or any kind of clean cloth into the wound.

2. Wrap snugly in a bandage. *See text on page 58 and accompanying figures.* An elastic bandage is preferred, if available.

If the bleeding is profuse

Apply a tourniquet. *See text on page 51 and accompanying figures.*

If the patient suffers from shock

See text on page 334.

What the Doctor Says Surprisingly enough, the barracuda will usually not attack a human swimmer or diver if left unmolested. On the other hand, a shark is very dangerous. A shark will be attracted by even a small quantity of blood. In the presence of a shark, a swimmer is best advised not to thrash about but to remain immobile, or at best move very slowly. It is safer to remain still than to beat a hasty retreat.

A killer whale is aggressive and destructive. If it is suspected that a killer whale is in the vicinity, it is best not to go into such waters. If a killer whale is spotted by a swimmer, he should move out of the area as promptly as he can manage; and on no account should he hang onto the side of a boat or allow his feet to dangle in the water.

A moray eel will usually not attack a human unless threatened by a swimmer whom the animal deems to be too close for comfort.

A spawning fish, who ordinarily would not attack a human, will bite if an individual encroaches on his territory.

BITES OF SNAKES AND SCORPIONS

CAUTION

- Do not permit the victim to walk or run.

- Do not give the victim alcohol in any form.

- Do not incise the wound unless the fang marks are clearly seen.

The fangs of a poisonous snake have hollow centers; they inject poison into the victim in the manner of a hypodermic syringe. When inspecting the victim, look for one to six fang marks in the skin. Each fang mark will appear as a puncture wound, resembling the penetration of the skin by a large needle.

Mild snake bite

Definition The snake did not make a clean strike; but only scratched the skin with one fang. In such a case, the pain will be minimal.

Moderate snake bite

Definition Fang marks causing local pain and swelling, but no general sick feeling.

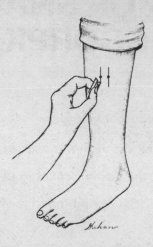

FIG. 74   *MAKING A LONGITUDINAL INCISION* *The incision is made over the point of entrance of the snake fang. Note that only a single longitudinal incision is performed over each point of entrance. Do not make an X-cut. The incision should be carried through the full thickness of the skin, down to the yellowish underlying fatty tissue.*

Severe snake bite

Definition   The appearance of fang marks with immediate excruciating pain, increasing swelling of the part, bluish discoloration, and a generalized sick feeling. Bloody spots, reddish or purple, will appear in the area surrounding the fang marks.

TREATMENT

1. Calm the victim.

2. Have the victim lie down.

3. Apply a venous tourniquet to an arm or leg between the bite and the heart. *See page 51.*

4. Do not permit the victim to walk.

5. If a doctor is not available, and if the effects of the bite are severe, incise the skin over the fang marks, as indicated below.

Technique

1. Keep the venous tourniquet in place.

2. Look for one to six fang marks, and make an incision *over each fang mark*. The incision should be longitudinal, and of ¼″ to ½″ (1 to 2 cms.) in length. Do not make cross incisions. *See Figure 74.*

3. Using a sharp knife or razor blade, cut through the entire thickness of the skin, until the underlying yellowish fatty tissue is seen. If possible, sterilize the instrument with alcohol or a flame. (The use of unsterilized instruments would be justified in an emergency situation.) Do not be concerned if the incision causes some bleeding.

4. After making cuts, squeeze the surrounding area gently in an attempt to get some of the venom out.

141

This poisonous material will be of a whitish-gray color, and be quite thick and sticky.

5. Cover with a sterile dressing or a clean cloth and bandage in place.

6. Transport the victim to a medical facility. Remember that the victim is to be carried.

7. If the victim has stopped breathing, apply mouth-to-mouth resuscitation. *See page 102*.

What the Doctor Says In some areas, a snake bitten native will amputate his own arm or leg on the spot, to avoid what he considers to be certain death. Yet it is known that snake venom stays in the local area for a long time, and only gradually seeps into the body.

Modern treatment consists of surgical removal of the venom.

The immediate application of a venous tourniquet is essential. The tourniquet can be allowed to stay on for two hours without being released, and up to four hours if removed for one minute out of every thirty. Sucking out the venom is *not* recommended. It accomplishes little, and may even introduce germs from the rescuer's mouth into the wound.

Naturally, it is wise to avoid snake territory known to be dangerous. But if one is obliged to enter such an area, good protective clothing—such as hiking boots, sturdy slacks, long sleeves, and gloves—is essential. One should not travel alone. It would be prudent to have transportation within call. Expeditions traveling in known snake areas should be equipped with a snake-bite kit which includes anti-venin for the particular varieties of poisonous snakes that infest the region. The kit should include a suction device to help remove the venom.

In a case of snake bite, it is wise to try to kill the snake so that it can be identified. This may be of prime interest to the physician.

Snake bites are not necessarily fatal. However, if the bite is not treated promptly, there may be a loss of skin and damage to deep tissue, or possible loss of part of a limb or even of the entire limb.

BLEEDING (INTERNAL)

Definition Bleeding deep in the tissues of the head, *see pages 271 and 287*, or in the abdomen, chest, or in the organs (liver, spleen, kidney); or from a ruptured blood vessel.

Symptoms These will vary with the location of the bleeding, as indicated below.

Internal bleeding, not obvious, may yet be quite serious, as in the rupture of a spleen or liver. The first-aider should suspect internal bleeding if there are signs of:

1. Severe blunt injury to the chest or abdomen, or evidence of a penetrating wound from a bullet, knife, or shrapnel. (A severely fractured rib may cause laceration of a lung, the spleen, or the left or right portion of the liver.)

2. Victim going into shock, *see page 334,* without obvious external bleeding.

3. Tenderness of the abdomen may indicate rupture of the liver, spleen, or intestine.

4. Blood in the urine. This may indicate rupture of a kidney.

5. Bloody vomit.

6. Gradual, delayed loss of consciousness, especially if the victim has initially been clear-minded after his injury. Such loss of consciousness suggests deep brain hemorrhage. *See pages 287 and 358.*

Any of the above conditions is very serious.

TREATMENT

Obvious Deep Bleeding in an extremity may be controlled by manual pressure. If this doesn't control the bleeding, then the use of pressure points, *see page 47 and accompanying figures*, or a tourniquet, *see page 51*, may be necessary.

Deep Internal Bleeding in a thigh may be severe enough to cause shock. *See page 334.*

For all of the above findings, there is little the first-aider can do. The victim should be transported to the nearest hospital in a horizontal position as rapidly as possible. An operation will likely be necessary.

BONE IN THROAT

CAUTION

- Do not give victim soft bread, or any other kind of food or drink, with the idea of having the bone swallowed or forced down the throat.

TREATMENT

1. Tell the victim to open his mouth, and urge him to cough out the bone.

2. If he doesn't succeed in doing this, ask the victim to open his mouth and stick out his tongue. Now, with the aid of a bright light—flashlight, if available—inspect the area.

3. Remove the bone by using your thumb and index finger, or by carefully using a tweezer.

If unable to locate and remove the bone

1. If the victim is an adult, have the victim bend over a chair with his head hanging down over the edge. *See Figure 111 on page 232.* If the victim is a child, lay him across your lap on his stomach. *See Figure 75.*

2. Tap lightly on the upper part of the victim's back.

3. If this light tapping does not dislodge the bone, rush victim to a doctor or a hospital.

If breathing is obstructed and victim seems to be choking

Follow instructions on *page 231* for first aid if object is stuck in throat. In the direst emergency, a stab tracheostomy may be necessary. *See page 115.*

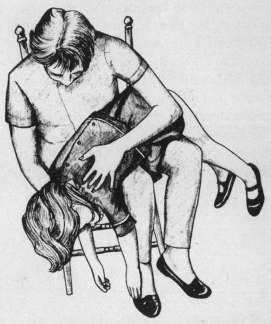

FIG. 75 *CHILD HELD ACROSS LAP TO DISLODGE FOREIGN BODY   Child is held head down, and back is lightly tapped.*

What the Doctor Says   In many instances, the victim can eliminate a fish bone if it is not too deeply embedded in the throat. If, however, the victim is suffocating—turning blue—and no professional help is available, the only option for a first-aider is an emergency stab tracheostomy. *See page 115.*

If possible, prevent the bone from falling into the stomach. That is why drinking water and eating bread to force the bone downward is inadvisable. It is true that a swallowed fish bone or a chicken bone may pass through the intestines, but there is always the danger of a sharp bone perforating the intestines and causing peritonitis. This condition is sometimes referred to as "fishbonitis."

If a fish bone or chicken bone is swallowed, observe the victim carefully for the next 48 hours. If abdominal discomfort develops, immediately consult a physician.

See Figure 113 on page 234. This is a drawing of the mouth, pharynx, windpipe, lungs and esophagus. It indicates diagramatically where a bone might be lodged.

BRUISE (CONTUSION)

Definition   An area which has been rendered tender because of a fall or a blow, In the early stages of the after-effects, no black and blue marks will be present.

TREATMENT

1. Remove any constricting clothing, such as shoes, socks, gloves, etc.

2. Apply ice bag, ice cubes, or cold compresses to area for eight hours or as long as practicable.

If the limb is possibly fractured

1. Splint the part. *See page 80.*

2. Bring victim to a medical facility.

What the Doctor Says   It is difficult at times to decide if there is an underlying fracture beneath the bruise. Only in a hospital where an X-ray can be obtained can the condition be determined.

In applying cold compresses, it is best to use two pieces of cloth, such as two napkins, two wash-cloths, or two towels. Place some ice cubes in an open vessel containing cold water. Place the cloths in the ice water until they become very cold. Squeeze out and apply one of the cloths to the bruised area. Allow the second cloth to remain in the ice water. As soon as the first cloth loses its coldness, remove it and apply the second cloth. Put the first cloth back on the ice. Continue this treatment until adequate relief is obtained.

Often, contusions are accompanied by scrapes and by open wounds. For the treatment of SKIN SCRAPES, *see page 338*. For the treatment of WOUNDS AND LACERATIONS, *see page 364*.

BULLET WOUNDS

CAUTION

- Do not give the victim any food or fluid.

TREATMENT

1. Control the bleeding. *See page 47.*

2. Apply a dressing at the point of entrance of the bullet, and at the point of exit. *See page 364.*

3. Rush the patient to a hospital. If injury occurs in country area where no hospital is available, rush victim to a doctor.

If the victim is in shock

See page 334.

If there is a head wound

1. Apply head bandage. *See page 74.*

2. Keep the victim flat on his back.

3. Rush the victim to a hospital.

If there is a fracture

Apply a splint. *See page 80.*

If there is a chest wound

1. Apply tight dressing as in sucking wound of the chest. *See page 163.*

2. Rush to a hospital.

If there is an abdominal wound

1. Apply a dressing. *See pages 58 and 364.*

2. Give nothing by mouth.

3. Rush to a hospital.

What the Doctor Says When a bullet hits a person, the point of entrance is marked by a small wound and the point of exit by a larger wound. The damage is dependent on a number of factors, such as the caliber of the bullet, the distance between the gun and the victim. It also depends on what tissues were damaged, such as bone, blood vessel, nerve, heart, lung, abdomen (kidney, spleen, liver, intestine). A flesh wound with a small caliber bullet, such as a 22, would not be too serious. But a 45-caliber bullet entering the chest or the abdomen or striking the thigh bone (femur) would be quite serious indeed. If a large artery is injured, the victim may bleed to death before any first aid could be applied. Multiple bullet wounds could be quite serious. A complete inspection of the entire body could determine the extent of the injury. *See page 22* on general inspection of a victim.

Shotgun injuries may be annoying but not serious. It is usually not possible for a surgeon to get all the lead out of the body, yet metal remaining in the body may not prove to be a serious problem. When the wound heals, the victim may function quite well with lead shot buried in his body. Even embedded bullets may remain quiescent indefinitely.

BURNS

Definition Burns may result from heat, chemicals, electricity, or radiation (X-rays or radioactive materials).

CAUTION

- Phosphorous burns require continuous washing down with large amounts of water while particles are being removed. Phosphorous tends to ignite on exposure to air.

Classification

1. *Minor Burns:*   Injuries which involve less than 10% of the body surface, and do not penetrate the entire thickness of the skin. (Exception: any burn of the face, or the hands, or the feet, or the genitals should be considered severe.)

2. *Severe Burns:*   Injuries which involve more than 10% of the body surface, and which penetrate the entire thickness of the skin. (Also any burn of the face, the hands, the feet or the genitals.) If in doubt as to whether a burn is minor or severe, regard the burn as severe.

TREATMENT

1. Remove the victim from the danger zone.

2. If clothing is on fire, extinguish the garments by smothering them with a blanket or coat, or by rolling the victim on the ground.

3. Pour cold water generously over the area of the burns.

4. If the face is burned, apply an iced cloth to the victim's face.

5. If the burn is chemical, apply water generously.

6. If the victim's clothes are soaked with the offending chemical, remove the victim's clothing.

7. The victim may be placed in a cold shower or a cold bath.

Treatment of Chemical Burns

If the first-aider can definitely identify the cause of a chemical burn to be an acid, then an alkali solution, such as bicarbonate of soda, could be applied after an irrigation with water. On the other hand, if a strong alkali such as lye is the cause, then a weak acid such as vinegar or acetic acid could be applied, after irrigation with water.

Treatment of Minor Burns

1. After first aid, a minor burn may be treated by an application of a thin layer of vaseline, butter, or some bland antibiotic ointment such as bacimycin, neosporin, furacin, or xeroform gauze. Apply gently.

2. Apply sterile gauze, preferably a non-adherent dressing such as telfa. If not available, use a clean cloth and wrap the wounded area snugly with a roller bandage.

Treatment of Major Burns

Caution For major burns, do not apply vaseline, butter, or ointment.

1. Cover the burn with sterile gauze or a clean cloth, and wrap the gauze in place. *Do not use an elastic bandage.* If the victim cannot be brought to a hospital or burn center promptly, wet the dressings with clear cold water.

2. If the victim's breathing becomes obstructed as a result of inhaled heat, emergency stab tracheostomy should be performed. *See page 115.*

3. Transport the victim to a hospital as rapidly as possible.

Electrical Burns

Caution The victim must be removed from contact with the electrical current before any first aid is applied. *See page 196.* Electrical burns generally cause more damage to the deeper tissues than may be apparent on the surface. A strong electrical current can destroy deep tissues.

Symptoms Electrocution may cause cessation of breathing and cardiac arrest.

TREATMENT

1. Initiate cardiopulmonary resuscitation. *See page 99.*

2. Summon a physician.

What the Doctor Says All burns are best treated by the immediate and continuous application of cold water or ice cloths. Ice cloths are particularly helpful in burns of the face. (The one exception is a phosphorous burn, as noted above.)

The fact that minor household burns will heal with either no treatment or a variety of simple home remedies has led to incorrect approaches in the first aid of severe burns. The application of butter or vaseline has no place in the treatment of severe burns.

For severe burns, a rapid method of estimating the percentage of body surface burned is the "Rule of Nines." *See Figures 76 and 77.*

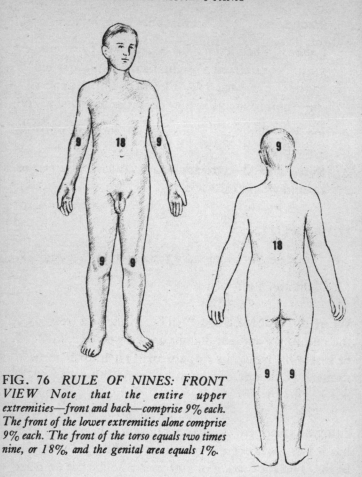

FIG. 76 RULE OF NINES: FRONT VIEW *Note that the entire upper extremities—front and back—comprise 9% each. The front of the lower extremities alone comprise 9% each. The front of the torso equals two times nine, or 18%, and the genital area equals 1%.*

FIG. 77 RULE OF NINES: REAR VIEW *Note that the entire head comprises 9%. The back equals two times nine, or 18%. The back of the legs equal 9% each. Sum for the entire body, front and back, equals 100%.*

Proper first aid for a severe burn involves the control of heat, flames, and chemicals, followed by an application of cold water and a clean cloth, and transportation—lying down—to a hospital.

However, if a burn is quite severe and involves a wide area of the body, the first-aider would be justified in getting the victim to a hospital as soon as possible, without applying any dressings.

Most first-aid books describe burns as first-degree, second-degree, and third-degree, dealing with the percentage of body surface involved and the nature of the burn. In practice, this type of classification has proved confusing. In this book, in order to simplify the treatment, burns are divided into minor burns and severe burns. Although no harm may develop from a minor burn being treated as a severe burn, the reverse is not true.

It should be kept in mind that burns may be complicated by the presence of fractures, or by asphyxiation, or through the blistering of the lining of the voice box (larynx), windpipe (trachea), bronchial tubes, and the lung tissue itself.

CHEST PAIN

Symptom Victim complains of strong pain in chest area. Victim clutches at chest.

CAUTION

- Give no cathartics (laxatives). Give no water. Give no alcoholic beverage.

TREATMENT

1. Rush victim to doctor or a hospital.

2. If the victim seems to be having a heart attack, *see page 289.*

What the Doctor Says Acute chest pain can be the result of indigestion caused by an intake of food to which the patient is allergic, or by the intake of poisonous food. Where the victim suffers from ulcers or disease of the gall bladder or pancreatitis, such pains may be present. The same is true of acute appendicitis or painful menstruation.

Certain medications, especially opiates, cause acute indigestion and vomiting.

While the chest pains in all of the above cases may be severe, the condition may or may not be serious. Just what the condition is must be diagnosed by a physician.

All the first-aider can do is to rush the victim to a medical facility as quickly as possible.

The chief worry in a case of acute chest pain is that the victim is suffering a heart attack. Diagnosing whether the pain is caused by a heart attack or by a simple case of indigestion is generally too difficult for the layman, but *see page 289* on HEART ATTACK.

A blood clot, suddenly lodging in the lungs, would cause severe chest pain. Clotted veins in the lower extremities or pelvis (phlebitis) precede the lung clot (pulmonary infarction). If this condition is suspected, the prompt care of a physician and the use of blood thinning medication (anti-coagulants) is essential.

CHEST WOUND

A chest wound, if it does not involve the lung cavity, should be treated like any other laceration. But if a wound involves the chest cavity, it is serious indeed and requires prompt action. Deep, internal bleeding may result.

If you can hear the sound of air being sucked into the chest with each breath, the victim is suffering from a

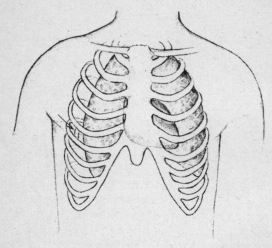

FIG. 78 *SUCKING WOUND OF CHEST (SEE ARROW)* *Air rushes into the lung cavity and collapses the lung. When the wound is sealed off, the air in the lung cavity is absorbed and the lung expands.*

sucking wound of the chest. *See Figure 78*. This may be caused by a bullet, a knife, a dagger, or a piece of metal.

CAUTION

- Do not remove a knife, a dagger or a piece of metal that remains plunged into the victim's chest. *See Figure 79*.

TREATMENT

1. Cover the wound with a generous quantity of sterile gauze or clean cloth. *See page 364 and Figure 80*.

2. Seal off the wound tightly by binding the dressing with adhesive or with a firm bandage around the chest, so that no air gets into the wound. *See Figure 80*.

FIG. 79 *KNIFE PLUNGED IN CHEST*

3. Rush the victim to a hospital.

FIG. 80 *SUCKING WOUND OF CHEST BEING SEALED First-aider places gauze on wound, and holds dressing in place with adhesive tape.*

What the Doctor Says The diaphragm is a dome-shaped thin muscle which divides the chest from the abdomen. In normal breathing, the diaphragm contracts and creates a vacuum between the lungs and the abdomen. Atmospheric pressure forces the lungs to expand with each breath.

If the chest wall has been perforated, the atmospheric pressure on both sides of the diaphragm becomes equalized, and consequently the lung collapses. This collapse prevents oxygen from being absorbed by the affected lung. The result is that the other lung, the uninjured one, must supply all the oxygen necessary to maintain life. A sucking wound of the chest which results in the collapse of one lung is a most serious injury and must be promptly corrected.

The objective of first aid is to seal off the open wound by whatever practical means are available. If the wound in the chest is large and is not easily closed, and cannot be easily sealed off, then the first-aider should stuff the opening with gauze or with a handkerchief or with a cloth before attempting to seal it off.

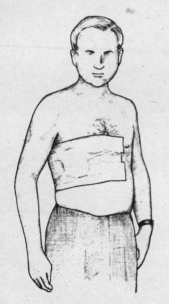

FIG. 81 *WOUND SEALED COMPLETELY WITH ADHESIVE TAPE*

It was cautioned not to remove a foreign body remaining plunged into the chest. In general, this is correct. But, a circumstance may exist in which there is no ambulance available, and it becomes necessary to transport the victim to a hospital in a private vehicle. In such an instance, the first aider should first prepare all the necessary material for sealing off a penetrating wound of the chest. After quickly removing the penetrating object, proceed immediately to seal off the chest. *See page 163.* Danger of deep, internal bleeding in the lung exists. Coughing up of blood is a sign of serious trouble. Treat for shock, if necessary. *See page 334.* Prompt transportation to a hospital is imperative.

CHILDBIRTH

CAUTION

- If an emergency childbirth occurs and the first-aider feels inadequate to handle it, he should not hold the mother's legs together to prevent delivery.

TREATMENT

If this is the mother's first delivery

1. Advise mother to breathe with her mouth open in short, panting breaths.

2. Mother should be placed on a bed with clean sheets. Position the mother so as to allow room on the bed for the baby to emerge. If no bed is available, place the mother on the floor or on the ground, spreading a clean sheet or cloth, and deliver the baby there.

3. Bend the mother's knees and hips, and separate the knees. *See Figure 82.*

4. Allow the head of the child to emerge slowly. *See Figure 83.* Use both your hands. Place one hand between the anus and the vagina of the mother. Place the other hand against the head of the infant. *See Figure 84.* Restrain the baby gently but sufficiently

to ease out the head gradually through the vagina. Avoid sudden emergence. *See Figure 85.*

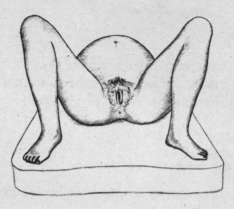

FIG. 82 *POSITION OF MOTHER IN PREPARATION FOR CHILDBIRTH*

FIG. 83 *HEAD OF CHILD BEGINNING TO EMERGE FROM VAGINA*

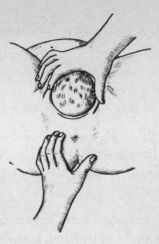

FIG. 84 FIRST-AIDER RESTRAINING EMERGENCE *He is placing one hand between the anus and the vagina of the mother, and his other hand against the head of the infant.*

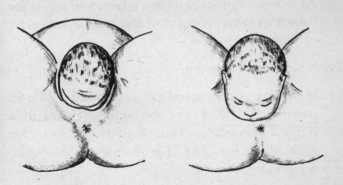

FIG. 85 HEAD OF BABY ALMOST OUT OF MOTHER

169

5. After the baby is completely out of the mother, immediately clean out the mouth of the infant with a sterile cloth, or with your fingers. Do this by sweeping the bent index finger wrapped in a small piece of gauze across the mouth, from one cheek to the other, and then out of the mouth.

6. Make certain that the umbilical cord is not wrapped around the baby's neck. If it is, gently unwrap it, using one finger. This must be performed gently without using force.

7. Support the newborn baby's body and head with one hand. With the other hand, grasp both legs of the infant firmly just above the ankles. *See Figure 86.*

8. Holding the baby over the bed, lift the baby up by its ankles so that its head is down and so that whatever fluids are in its mouth will drain out.

9. At this point, most newborn infants will cry. If the baby does not cry, snap your fingers against the soles of the baby's feet.

10. Note time of delivery.

11. If a doctor or a hospital can be reached within 10 minutes, do NOT cut the umbilical cord. If a hospital cannot be reached, tie off the umbilical cord as shown in *Figure 87*. Tie off twice, as illustrated, using string or cord.

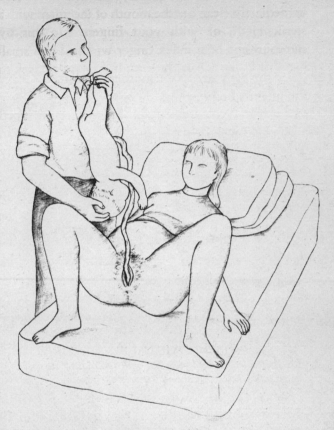

FIG. 86 *BABY EMERGING FROM WOMB Holding new born infant, the first-aider grasps the newborn infant firmly by his ankles so that whatever fluids are in the infant's mouth will drain out.*

171

12. Do not pull on the umbilical cord to hasten emergence of the afterbirth (placenta). Do not be alarmed if a moderate amount of blood emerges from the vagina.

13. Place the baby across the mother's abdomen. Cover the infant's body with a sheet.

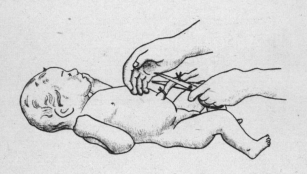

FIG. 87 *CUTTING THE UMBILICAL CORD*
The first-aider has made two ties with cord. Using scissors, he now cuts the umbilical cord between the two ties.

If the mother has previously given birth

Then, even if the contractions are further apart than two minutes, and even if the baby's head is not showing at the vagina, take the mother's word for it if she says that she is about to give birth.

If the top of the baby's shoulder emerges first

Apply a gentle pull on the head of the baby, directing the head toward the ceiling. Use both hands. *See Figure 88.* This will enable the other shoulder to slide out gently. When both shoulders are out, the rest of the body will come out easily, as the mother continues with her contractions.

FIG. 88 *ASSISTING BABY'S SHOULDER OUT OF VAGINA First-aider is applying a gentle pull on the head of the baby, directing the head toward the ceiling. He is using both hands. This enables the shoulder inside the vagina to slide out gently.*

If the mother vomits

Keep her body flat with chin up. Keep head turned sharply to one side. *See Figure 101 on page 209.* If possible, place a pillow or bolster or any suitable object under the mother's buttocks, so as to prevent any vomitus from going into her lungs.

If the mother continues to bleed profusely

This is a danger signal and should be treated as shock. *See page 334.* Get the patient to a hospital or summon immediate medical aid.

If the buttocks of the infant appear first at the vagina (Breech Birth)

1. Permit the mother to push out her baby as far as the baby's navel. *See Figure 89.*

2. Be sure the navel is pointed towards the floor. *See Figure 90.*

3. If it isn't, gently and slowly rotate the baby's body so the navel points to the floor. *See Figure 91.*

4. Grasp the baby's legs firmly above the ankles and gently assist the emergence of the infant by pressing the mother's lower abdomen with your other hand to help the head come out. Do this slowly, deliberately, and gently, holding the baby's legs firmly in your hand all the time. *See Figure 92.*

5. Do not let the baby slip to the floor. *See Figure 93.*

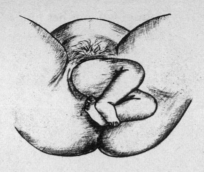

FIG. 89 *BREECH DELIVERY First Step The first-aider permits the mother to push out her baby as far as the infant's navel.*

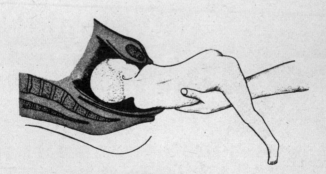

FIG. 90 *BREECH DELIVERY Second Step The first-aider attempts to point the infant's navel toward the floor.*

175

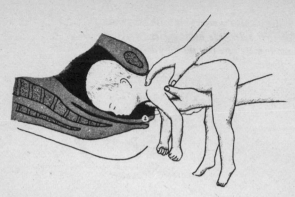

FIG. 91 BREECH DELIVERY *Third Step The first-aider rotates the infant's body to make sure that the navel is pointed toward the floor.*

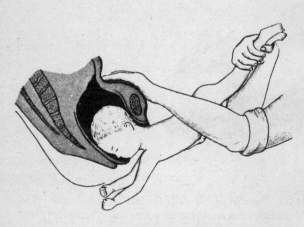

FIG. 92 BREECH DELIVERY *Fourth Step The first-aider grasps the baby's legs above the ankles and gently assists emergence. He presses the mother's lower abdomen to help the head come out.*

176

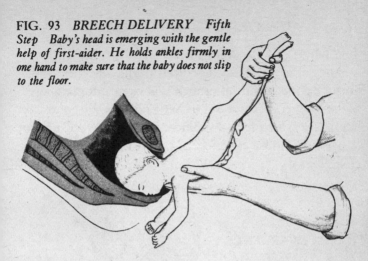

FIG. 93 *BREECH DELIVERY Fifth Step Baby's head is emerging with the gentle help of first-aider. He holds ankles firmly in one hand to make sure that the baby does not slip to the floor.*

CARE OF BABY AFTER BIRTH

CAUTION

- Do not spank or shake the baby.

If infant does not breathe nor cry

1. Lay infant flat on bed.

2. Keep the baby's chin up and its head back.

3. Compress chest gently.

If baby does not start to breathe

Use gentle mouth-to-mouth respiration. *See page 102.*

177

DELIVERY OF AFTERBIRTH

The delivery of the afterbirth will usually occur 15 or 20 minutes after the baby has been born. The first-aider must be patient. The afterbirth will come out gradually, as the mother forces it out of her vagina as she contracts her muscles. *See Figure 94.* These contractions will not be as painful as those experienced before the delivery of the child.

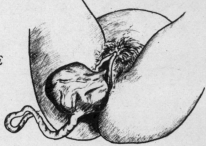

FIG. 94 *EMERGENCE OF AFTERBIRTH*

After the placenta has been delivered, the first-aider should proceed as follows:

1. Place your hand on the uterus (womb) which is located deep in the midline of the lower abdomen.

2. Compress the uterus firmly, but do not use undue force. *See Figure 95.*

3. Firmness will gradually develop under your hand.

4. Continue to do this for the next 30 minutes, making sure that the uterus becomes firm.

178

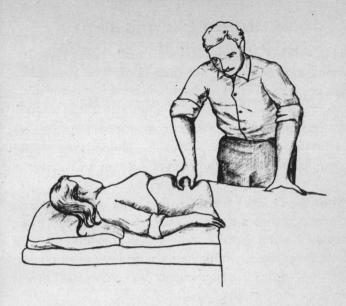

FIG. 95 *COMPRESSING THE UTERUS The first-aider grasps the mother's womb in his hand, and compresses the uterus firmly.*

If the uterus becomes soft under your hand

Massage the uterus and continue using one hand to press the uterus down until it becomes firm again.

If the uterus, having once become firm, softens again

Additional massage should be applied until the uterus stays firm. This is easily felt in the compressing hand.

179

IF MOTHER IS GIVING BIRTH FOLLOWING ACCIDENTAL INJURY

If mother is in shock

1. Follow instructions given on *page 334*.

2. Summon an ambulance. If condition is not so severe as to warrant an ambulance, phone hospital and inform them that a pregnant woman will arrive.

What the Doctor Says   A first-aider who has had no experience with a delivery may become alarmed if the mother's water breaks and he sees a sudden gush of colorless or slightly pink fluid, containing a small amount of blood, come out of her vagina. This is normal. There is no cause for concern.

Another situation where the first-aider may be unduly worried is where the mother is involved in some kind of accident. In most instances where a prospective mother is injured, the unborn child will remain unhurt. Premature delivery will not necessarily occur. A pregnant woman involved in an accident may pass urine at the time of the accident, but this is not important and may be due mainly to nervous tension. Such wetting should not be confused with the "breaking of the waters" which occurs previous to childbirth.

In severe accidents, it is possible that a mother will be near death and that her life cannot be saved. Nevertheless, the life of the infant may be preserved through Cesarean section.

CONVULSION

Definition A convulsion is a seizure caused by disorderly discharges of electrical action in the brain cells producing jerky muscular movements.

Symptoms The victim suffers from loss of consciousness. His eyes may roll; he may be frothing from the mouth; he may clench his teeth; and his muscles may twitch jerkily. If he was standing, the victim may have fallen to the ground. He may be losing urine; may be losing stool; and may be moaning.

TREATMENT

1. *See* EPILEPSY, *page 199.*

2. Obtain medical assistance promptly.

What the Doctor Says Convulsion in an adult may be caused by a head injury with brain damage, or by a brain tumor, or by epilepsy. Diagnosis must be made by a physician.

A convulsion in an infant may be caused by high fever. Immediate first aid is the same as for epilepsy, but a doctor should be consulted. Aspirin and tepid water baths will help bring down the temperature and, for the moment, help prevent further convulsions. The proper diagnosis, treatment, and use of antibiotics must be directed by a physician.

CROUP

Definition   A form of laryngitis in infants.

Symptoms   A rough, hoarse cough sounding somewhat like the bark of a dog. Breathing is difficult.

CAUTION

- If croup is accompanied by a fever of 102 degrees Fahrenheit or more (39° C.), seek medical aid promptly.

TREATMENT

1. Fill the bathroom with steam from the bathtub or sink. Place the child in the room. Prompt relief should be experienced.

2. Steam the child's sleeping room, in preparation for the victim's return.

3. If necessary, improvise a technique of steaming by making a tent in the child's crib and filling the tent with vapor from an electric inhalator or from boiling water. Be careful to avoid scalding the child.

4. If no improvement is evident within the hour, call a doctor.

What the Doctor Says Croup can occur with or without fever. Spasmodic croup without fever may develop suddenly at night in an infant who has not been particularly sick during the day. The child wakes up with a hoarse, barking cough and finds breathing difficult. Prompt application of moist air, by one means or another, will afford relief.

If boiling water is used, be cautious about avoiding accident from scalding. An adult should stay in the same room as the infant all night for surveillance. Once croup has made its appearance, steam should be employed for a few nights in succession.

If croup is associated with fever and with a chest cold, call a physician for accurate diagnosis and treatment. Antibiotics may be necessary.

DIABETIC COMA
(Acidosis or Ketosis)

Definition   A condition in which sugar is not properly metabolized by the diabetic, resulting in severe acidosis and coma.

CAUTION

- Do not mistakenly treat diabetic coma as insulin shock. *See pages 298-300.* If in doubt, and if the victim is alert enough to swallow, give the victim either two teaspoonfuls of sugar in a glass of water or two lumps of sugar. An erroneous administration of sugar will do no harm, but would be greatly beneficial if insulin shock were present. If no response is noted within five minutes, do nothing further.

TREATMENT

1. If vomiting occurs, have the victim lie flat on his back. *See text on page 211 and Figure 101.*

2. Rush victim to a hospital.

What the Doctor Says There is no specific treatment that the first-aider should administer in this situation. Since diabetic coma is the result of uncontrolled diabetes mellitus, the physician will be required to render intensive care. This may take anywhere from hours to days.

Treatment may demand intravenous therapy, the administration of insulin, and careful and continuous monitoring of blood and urine changes.

Diabetic acidosis may rapidly develop as the result of an infection in some part of the body. If this is not treated, the diabetes may get out of control and the victim may become groggy and drift into coma.

All diabetics should wear an identifying bracelet or pendant. *See page 28.*

DIARRHEA

Definition   Frequent passage of loose, unformed stools.

Symptoms   The victim is stricken with frequent bowel movements of loose stools. As many as 50 watery or bloody bowel movements may occur in a single day. The victim experiences abdominal discomfort with a griping sensation, loss of appetite, and nausea. Vomiting may be present. The victim suffers from fatigue. His muscles may ache. Fever may be present.

IMPORTANT   A bloody diarrhea may indicate a serious condition. Victim should immediately be transported, lying down, to a hospital.

CAUTION

- No food or liquids are to be given to the victim.

TREATMENT

1. The victim should be made to lie down.

2. Reassure the victim that he will get well.

3. Arrange for medical assistance.

What the Doctor Says   There are many causes of diarrhea. Some attacks may be mild and short-lived.

Others may come without warning, severe and disabling. Some cases of diarrhea may be caused by a serious disease, such as amebic dysentery or cholera.

Diarrhea may be the result of bacillary dysentery, amebic dysentery, viral gastro-enteritis, food poisoning, acute intestinal allergy, regional ileitis, ulcerative colitis, or food indiscretion as represented by excessive drinking of alcoholic beverages. Diarrhea may also result from psychological stress caused by fear or shock. Amebic dysentery is generally caused by contaminated food, and usually occurs in tropical areas. Antibiotics, rest, intravenous fluids and intestinal sedatives comprise the treatment.

The patient who expects to travel to the Tropics may take the preventive step of being vaccinated against typhoid, paratyphoid, and cholera.

Botulism is a form of food poisoning incurred by eating contaminated food. The usual causes are home-canned fruits, vegetables, fish or meat which have not been completely sterilized. The onset generally occurs somewhere between 12 to 30 hours after the ingestion of the offending substance. In severe forms of botulism, the victim may be stricken with paralysis. *See* FOOD POISONING on *page 220*.

Where a person is intensely allergic to certain foods, he may develop all the symptoms associated with diarrhea. A person so stricken should consult a physician to determine just what his allergy is, and so learn to avoid the offending substance.

DROWNING

TREATMENT

Apply mouth-to-mouth breathing. *See page 102.* Rescuer can begin this in shallow water by bending the victim's head over his knee and applying mouth-to-mouth breathing. *See Figure 96.*

IMPORTANT Start mouth-to-mouth breathing before trying to get water out of lungs.

If the victim vomits

Lower his head and turn the head to one side. *See Figure 101 on page 209.*

If no pulse is present

Seek medical attention promptly.

What the Doctor Says When a person has drowned in salt water, a frothy, bloody stained fluid may emerge from his nose and mouth. If the victim has no pulse at the time of his rescue, his chance of survival is slim, but the first-aider should make an attempt to revive him because cases have been known where victims have been saved even after exhibiting these dismaying symptoms.

Drowning is the result of water entering the lungs and blocking the normal intake of oxygen. An individual can survive a lack of oxygen for four minutes. If the oxygen deprivation extends beyond this time, irreversible changes develop which lead to rapid death. Therefore, quick action is of the essence. Prompt rescue and immediate efforts at resuscitation are imperative.

FIG. 96   *ADMINISTERING MOUTH-TO-MOUTH BREATHING IN SHALLOW WATER*

It is not necessary to position the victim so as to remove the water from his lungs. Mouth-to-mouth breathing should be started immediately. But if the victim's condition is satisfactory and there is time, removal of water from the lungs can be done by draping the victim over a barrel, face down. Do this only if such a

189

barrel or bench is right at hand. Otherwise, don't waste time looking for these objects, but proceed as soon as possible with mouth-to-mouth breathing.

Continue your attempt at resuscitation for at least one hour, or until a doctor has pronounced the victim to be dead.

But of course, what is most important is the avoidance of such accidents. Write to your local American National Red Cross. This organization publishes booklets which contain prudent recommendations about sports.

To prevent trouble:

1. Learn how to swim proficiently.

2. Do not swim in deep water unless you are accompanied by a friend who is a good swimmer and who knows the elements of lifesaving.

3. Practice lifesaving techniques.

4. Do not attempt a distance swim unless a boat which contains a life preserver follows you all the way.

DRUG OVERDOSE

Definition   The effect of a dose of drugs larger than the victim's body can tolerate, such as:

1. An overdose of a normally prescribed sleeping pill or tranquilizer.

2. An overdose of heroin.

3. An overdose of amphetamines.

TREATMENT

If the victim is conscious

1. Do not threaten him. Talk to him reassuringly, and try to calm him.

2. Keep the victim warm by covering him.

If the victim is unconscious

1. Turn the victim on his side.

2. Turn the victim's head to one side. This will permit secretions to flow out of the victim's mouth, and will not obstruct his breathing.

3. Attempt to stimulate the victim by calling out his name. Shake him gently; slap him gently; or pinch him gently. Such procedure will indicate the depth

of the victim's unconsciousness. If the victim reacts with bodily movements and utters some sounds, one can conclude the coma is not too deep.

4. If breathing has ceased, apply mouth to mouth breathing. *See page 102.*

5. If cardiac arrest or there is a severe irregularity in the heart rhythm, *see page 99,* external cardiac massage will be necessary.

6. If convulsions are present and the victim is thrashing about, protect the victim against self-inflicted damage. *See* CONVULSION, *page 181,* and EPILEPSY, *page 199.*

7. If victim is violent or dangerous, bodily restraint may be necessary.

8. If you cannot identify the drug responsible for the episode, bring a sample of the drug or its container to the physician for identification.

9. Look around the area for a possible suicide note.

10. If it is known that the victim has very recently swallowed a large amount of sedatives, and if immediate hospital or medical care is not available, and if the individual is fully conscious, induce vomiting. *See page 319.*

11. Transport the victim to a hospital. Two first-aiders should accompany the victim.

DRUNKENNESS

Definition   Toxic effects of excessive intake of alcoholic beverages, causing boisterous, combative behavior, confusion, restlessness, unsteadiness, stupor, convulsions, and coma. The intensity of the symptoms will depend on the degree of the alcoholic poisoning.

CAUTION

- Do not permit the victim to imbibe any further alcoholic beverages.

- Do not give the victim any medicine, or any kind of food or fluid.

- Do not try to "walk" the victim.

Symptoms of Acute Alcoholism:

1. Staggering gait.

2. Slurred speech.

3. A decrease in pain sensation (in response, for example, to a pin prick).

4. Decreased movement of body, or no movement at all.

5. Unconsciousness, stupor, or coma.

6. Severe retching and/or vomiting of blood.

7. Loss of blood from the anus.

8. Signs of shock. *See page 334.*

9. Evidence of head injury. *See page 287.*

Symptoms of Delirium Tremens (DT's):

1. Restlessness; irritability; sleeplessness.

2. Aversion to food.

3. Shaking tremors; convulsions.

4. Moist skin.

5. Bloodshot eyes.

6. Flushed face.

7. Hallucinations.

What the Doctor Says   There is little that a first-aider can do beyond arranging for proper medical assistance.

The mere odor of alcohol on the breath does not prove intoxication. The victim may be suffering from a head injury, or he may have imbibed an alcoholic beverage while on antabuse therapy (antabuse is a drug used to correct alcoholism). During its use, the ingestion of an alcoholic beverage is forbidden. If an individual under treatment drinks an alcoholic beverage, some serious effects, such as mental confusion, severe cardiac symptoms, shock, lack of knowledge as to whereabouts, or even unconsciousness may result. Antidote therapy is usually prescribed on a card carried by the individual taking antabuse.

An alcoholic may conceal the odor of alcohol on his breath, and even deny that he has been drinking. Not infrequently, the victim is suffering from the combined toxic effects of a sleeping pill or a tranquilizer as well as an alcoholic beverage. This combination can cause serious effects. The "shakes," seeing things that are not there (hallucinations), and convulsions are signs of impending delirium tremens (DT's). Such symptoms indicate that medical attention is imperative. Following heavy drinking, DT's represent a withdrawal reaction.

If the victim is unconscious, only a physician can determine the cause. That cause may not be acute alcoholic intoxication; the condition may be due to a head injury, *see page 287,* or to diabetes, *see page 184,* or to brain tumor, or to severe pneumonia, or other severe infection.

When transporting an unconscious victim, keep his body flat, handle him carefully, close his eyelids, *see page 205,* and keep the body warm by covering with a blanket.

Unfortunately, alcoholism is universally prevalent, even among persons below the age of fifteen. It is a leading cause of death, and should be recognized and treated as a disease. A high suicide rate occurs among middle-aged alcoholics.

ELECTRICAL BURN AND SHOCK

CAUTION

- If the victim has to be pulled or pushed away from a live wire, use insulated gloves. Push or pull him out with a wooden stick or a wooden cane, or any non-conductor of electricity, such as rubber, leather or cloth. *See Figure 97.*

- The first-aider should be careful not to touch the victim with naked hands because he will run the risk of electrical shock to himself.

- Do not give the victim any stimulants, such as Spirits of Ammonia, alcoholic beverages, or coffee. You may, however, give him plain water.

- Do not disturb the victim by unnecessary questioning, bodily manipulation, or noise.

TREATMENT

1. Remove the victim—and yourself—from further danger from the source of the electricity.

2. Shut off the electrical current or remove the open fuse.

196

3. Keep the victim warm.

4. Rush the victim to a hospital.

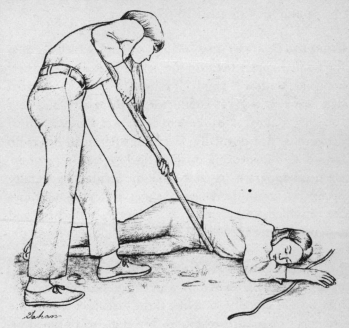

FIG. 97 *FIRST-AIDER PUSHING VICTIM OFF LIVE ELECTRICAL WIRE* First-aider is using a wooden pole.

If the victim is not breathing

Apply mouth-to-mouth breathing. *See page 102.* Continue artificial respiration until you can get the victim to a hospital.

197

If the victim seems to be suffering from heart failure

A trained person should apply external massage. *See page 106*. As long as some heart action is present, continue with artificial respiration.

What the Doctor Says   Most accidents which occur in the home happen because someone touches an electrical appliance with wet hands. It cannot be over-emphasized that water is a great conductor of electricity and that handling electrical equipment with wet hands is most dangerous. But normally, electrical equipment offers no hazard if it conforms to municipal codes. It is where electrical apparatus is faulty that the accidents generally occur. For example, when washing or drying machines are installed, they must be properly attached and grounded. An experienced electrician should perform the installation.

When a person suffers electrical shock, he may stop breathing and his heart may waiver in its beating. Prompt first aid can literally save life. If the first aider applies the principles of mouth-to-mouth breathing as outlined on *page 99*, he will be able to sustain the individual if the victim has not been totally electrocuted. The resuscitation must be started within four minutes if it is to be successful. If the first aid is too late, the victim may survive as a "vegetable"—maintaining his life and limb but paralyzed and unable to speak—a living death.

EPILEPSY

Symptoms The victim often loses consciousness and control of his muscles. Sometimes the victim experiences an aura—some sign which comes to him either visually or through hearing or through smelling, which indicates that an attack is imminent. If the victim tells you that he is about to have an attack, ease him gently to a lying-down position with his back on the floor, or at least ease him gently into a soft chair. Just prior to the seizure, there may be a short, hoarse cry, which may be followed immediately by a fall to the floor, unless the first-aider prevents this fall by prompt action. A fit follows. The victim's muscles tighten, and then he lapses into jerky, twitchy movements, and generally froths at the mouth.

TREATMENT

1. The first-aider must keep calm; he cannot stop the seizure. If the individual thrashes about, do not try to interfere with his movements in any way.

2. Clear the surrounding area of objects to prevent the victim's incurring injury.

3. Place a folded handkerchief between his teeth to keep him from biting his tongue. *See Figure 98.* Do

199

not place a pencil or a piece of rigid metal in the folded handkerchief: these may break a tooth.

FIG. 98 *WEDGING FOLDED CLOTH BETWEEN TEETH OF VICTIM* *The first-aider has thrust a folded piece of cloth into the mouth of the victim to keep him from biting his tongue.*

4. Allow 10 minutes for the fit to subside. If you are dealing with a known epileptic, it is not necessary to call a doctor. However, if the attack is followed by another major seizure, if the attack lasts more than 10 minutes, or if the victim is pregnant, seek medical aid promptly.

What the Doctor Says Epilepsy is a name covering a number of disorders of the nervous system in which brain cells discharge too much electrical energy. Symptoms vary from person to person. An infant may develop a convulsion through high fever, a convulsion may follow a head injury, or a convulsion may be a manifestation of a brain tumor. Such convulsions will resemble an epileptic convulsion. But the run-of-the-mill epileptic convulsion is a transient episode without untoward effect.

EYE INJURED BY CHEMICAL

TREATMENT

1. Hold the victim's eyelids open with index finger and thumb of one hand.

2. Slowly pour lukewarm water over the eyeball. Continue for five minutes. Pour slowly. Do not use a forceful stream. *See Figure 99*.

3. Rush the victim to a hospital.

What the Doctor Says   Chemical burns of the eye, caused by a lye or an acid, demand prompt attention if the victim's eyesight is to be preserved. The damaging agent must be promptly diluted by rinsing the affected part. Rinsing should be immediate and continuous for at least five minutes. Ideally, a clean vessel with a spout should be used; but if this is not available, any container or faucet or hose may be used—even one cup of water after another. After the first aid is completed, the victim should be promptly brought to a hospital or doctor.

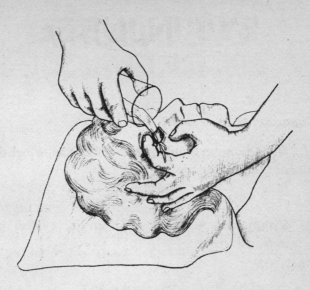

FIG. 99 *IRRIGATING THE EYE* *The first-aider is shown prying eyelids apart using two fingers of one hand. With the other, he pours water directly on the affected eyeball.*

EYE INJURY

Contusion of the Eyeball

Definition   A blunt blow to the eyeball which does not cause a rupture.

Symptoms   A severe pain in the eyeball plus impaired vision.

CAUTION

- Do not apply ice or an iced cloth directly to the eye. Use only a cold-water compress.

- Do not test for pain by pressing on the eyeball.

- Do not allow the victim to lie flat.

TREATMENT

1. Have the victim sit up. If he must lie down, prop up his head with a makeshift pillow.

2. Apply a soft cloth, dipped in cold water and squeezed out, to the victim's closed eyelid.

3. If severe pain in the eyeball does not subside in five minutes, transport the victim to a physician, who

preferably is an ophthalmologist. A physician's subsequent care is also necessary.

4. If vision is blurred, transport the victim to a physician. Test his vision by asking him whether he can recognize the face of another individual at a distance of six feet (two meters). If the victim wears glasses, test him with his glasses on.

5. Cover the injured eye with an eyeshield, or with the victim's cupped hand. Do not use a bandage or an eye pad. If a paper cup is available this can be used as an improvised shield by cutting it down to two thirds its height and placing it upside down over the injured eye. Fix in place with two crossed strips of adhesive tape.

If the eyeball is perforated

Where the eyeball is perforated by a sharp object, the danger of loss of vision is extreme, and the victim should be rushed to a hospital.

If the patient is unconscious and the eyelids are open

To prevent injury to the eye, gently close his eyelids with your hands. If they open again, tape them closed with adhesive or Scotch tape. *See Figure 100.*

If the victim's eyeglasses have been broken, and the glass gets into his eye

1. Do not rub the eye.

2. Allow glass to fall out, if it does so without manipulation.

3. Cover the eye gently with gauze.

4. Rush victim to a doctor or hospital.

If the victim has suffered complete loss of vision

1. Do not attempt first aid.

2. Rush victim to a hospital.

FIG. 100   *EYELIDS OF UNCONSCIOUS PATIENT TAPED CLOSED*

If the victim is suffering from a hemorrhage of the lids and the eyeball

1. Do not attempt first aid.

2. Rush victim to a hospital.

What the Doctor Says Eyeball injuries may be caused by a fist in a brawl, or by the victim's impaling his eye on a sharp object like an umbrella, or by the victim's being hit by a ball, or by foreign objects, such as pieces of metal, small or large. Serious deep bleeding may result from an injury from a blunt object and may even require an operation.

A blunt injury to an eyeball may cause temporary sharp pain. If this subsides in five minutes and if vision is not impaired, the chances are that no severe injury has resulted.

There is still a danger, however, that a delayed reaction may develop, such as bleeding into the eyeball, a detached retina, traumatic glaucoma, or some shift in the position of the lens. Hence, it is wise to observe the victim closely. If in doubt, transport him to a physician, preferably to an eye specialist (an ophthalmologist).

Eye injuries may be of little account, or may be of the utmost seriousness. In any kind of injury to the eye, the victim may suffer pain, burning, or spasm of the eyelids in which the eyelids flutter. The first-aider would do well in all such cases to get the victim to a medical facility. In some instances instrumentation is needed. The eye will have to be anesthetized. Special drops may be placed in the eye to reveal the foreign body and if imbedded, the foreign body will have to be removed with special instruments.

FAINTING

TREATMENT

1. Ease the victim down slowly to the floor and have him lie on his back.

2. Turn the patient's head to one side so that if he vomits, the material will drain out of his mouth and will not clog his lungs. *See Figure 101.* If vomiting occurs, it would be even of greater benefit to turn the victim face down.

3. Loosen any tight clothing around the victim's neck or chest.

4. Feel the victim's pulse. *See Figure 7 on page 42.* Count the number of pulse beats per minute. Seventy-two is average for a person at rest. In fainting, the pulse may be slow or rapid; it is rarely normal. Note the number of pulse beats per minute for future reference in reporting to a physician.

5. Count the victim's respirations. Fifteen to 20 breaths per minute is average. In fainting, breathing may be shallow, slow, or rapid. Again, note the number of respirations per minute for future reference in reporting to a physician.

If the victim emerges from his faint

Do not allow him to stand up or sit down. Keep him lying in a recumbent position for at least 10 minutes in order to facilitate full recovery.

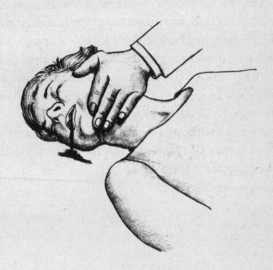

FIG. 101 *PREVENTING VOMITUS FROM ENTERING LUNGS The first-aider sharply turns victim's head to one side.*

If respiration or pulse are below normal

Give the victim smelling salts, such as Spirits of Ammonia. This will cause a sharp reaction which

209

may waken the victim. Do not persist in holding the salts to the nostrils, but if the victim has been aroused, give him a quick whiff of the salts at intervals. If the patient is not aroused at one whiff, the first-aider should apply a second whiff.

Spirits of Ammonia comes in two forms and may be obtained from any pharmacist: (1) It is packaged in a wide-mouthed bottle with a glass stopper. To use, remove the stopper and place open mouth of bottle directly under the nostrils; (2) It also comes as an ampoule covered with cloth. *See Figure 2, number 5, on page 32.* To use, break the ampoule by holding it between the thumb and index fingers of both hands. *See Figure 102.* Place the ampoule directly under the nostrils. *See Figure 103.*

FIG. 102 *BREAKING AN AMPOULE OF SMELLING SALTS Using index finger and thumb, grasp the ends of the ampoule, one in each hand, and with a quick snap, break the glass.*

FIG. 103 *APPLYING AN AMPOULE OF SMELLING SALTS The first-aider places the broken ampoule under the victim's nose.*

If the victim does not respond to the above treatment

Medical help should be immediately sought.

If the victim vomits

Place the victim face down on the floor so that the vomitus can proceed from his mouth without obstruction. If the victim cannot be turned completely around, then make sure to turn the victim's head to one side. *See Figure 101.*

What the Doctor Says   Fainting may result from any cause which results in diminished flow of blood to the

211

brain. When a person suddenly loses consciousness, it may be due to a simple fainting spell or to a much more serious condition. Only a physician can determine the cause.

Fainting may be caused by psychic disturbances, shock, seeing blood, hearing unpleasant news, spending a long time in a given position, suffering extreme pain, etc.

FIG. 104 *PERSON WHO FEELS FAINT, LYING ON HIS BACK His feet have been placed on a chair so that they are higher than his head.*

Where a person announces that he is likely to faint, the best thing to do is to lay him on his back and raise his legs above his head by placing them on a low chair or bench or any other elevation, such as a pile of books or a box. *See Figure 104.* If a woman is involved and she finds this position embarrassing, ask her to sit on a chair and lower her head between her knees. *See Figure 105.*

The most important thing to keep in mind is that a victim recovers promptly from a simple faint. If he does not, lose no time in obtaining medical aid.

FIG. 105 *PREVENTING FAINTING SPELL BY BENDING HEAD BETWEEN KNEES*

FALLING THROUGH ICE

If alone

The victim should keep his body as horizontal as possible and kick furiously until he scoots his body out of the water and onto the ice into a prone position. *He should not try to climb out vertically.*

If being rescued

The rescuer should never stand up to aid the victim. Instead, the rescuer must crawl on a 14-to-18-foot (4 to 5 meters) board. If no board is available, a human chain can be formed, each person holding the ankles of the person in front. When the victim has a firm hold, or is firmly held by the rescuer, the human chain wriggles back toward safety, dragging the victim along in a prone position.

Once the victim is securely on land, remove his wet clothing, wrap him in blankets, and if possible, arrange for a warm—*not hot*—bath.

If the victim had been drowning, initiate resuscitation. *See page 188.*

To avoid an emergency situation, an adult supervisor should see that children

1. Skate in a shallow region where the depth of the water beneath the ice is no more than waist high.

2. Skate with at least one companion.

3. Skate during the day, only.

4. Check the depth of the ice.

   a. Ice two inches (5 cms.) thick can hold one person.

   b. A uniform depth of four inches (10 cms.) is needed to support a group.

   c. A minimum depth of seven to eight inches (18 to 20 cms.) is needed to support a snowmobile or ice boat.

Look for these indicators of weak ice

1. Dark-colored ice.

2. An underlying spring of moving water.

3. Air pockets which have formed in an area where water is being or has been drawn off.

FEVER IN INFANTS

CAUTION

- Do not use alcohol in bathing a fevered infant. The vapor will be inhaled and may have a toxic effect.

TREATMENT

1. Administer a lukewarm bed bath, using a wash cloth or its equivalent. Bathe one part at a time, first the face, then one upper extremity, then neck and chest, etc. Keep all other parts covered.

2. Give aspirin. Dose: grains 1¼ (80 mgs) for each year up to age 4, at which time dose would be 5 grains (320 mgs).

3. Summon a physician.

What the Doctor Says   A fever in an infant may go as high as 105 degrees Fahrenheit (41 degrees Centigrade). Besides weakening the child, a high fever may cause convulsions. In the absence of a physician, the recommended treatment will suffice as an emergency measure.

FISH HOOK IN FLESH

TREATMENT

1. Remove the hook.

2. Cleanse the wound with soap and water.

3. Dry with sterile gauze.

4. Apply antibiotic ointment. If this is not available, soak the affected part in a solution of one tablespoon of salt placed in a glass of clean water. If no fresh water is available, use clean sea water. Soak the wound for 10 minutes.

5. Dress the wound. *See page 58.*

If the affected part starts to swell and pain develops

Get the victim to a hospital.

If the hook cannot be easily removed

1. Make a small opening in the skin by using a sterilized needle, or a sterilized razor blade, or a sharp sterilized knife. Make a cut into the flesh from the point of the barb to the shank of the fish hook so that the hook can be removed. *See Figure 106.*

2. The cut should be made only deep enough to effect extraction.

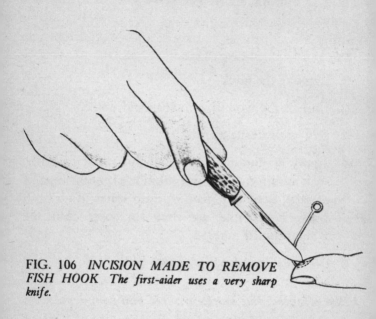

FIG. 106 *INCISION MADE TO REMOVE FISH HOOK* The first-aider uses a very sharp knife.

If the hook is embedded too deeply to be removed by the above technique

1. Push the hook further into the flesh. *See Figure 107.*

2. Then cut off the tip of the protruding fish hook with its barb. Use heavy scissors or wire snippers.

3. Then withdraw the fish hook.

What the Doctor Says If a fish hook is deeply embedded in the flesh, removal by a first-aider may be difficult. Medical assistance should, when possible, be obtained. However, when fishing in a remote area where medical assistance is not available, then in order to remove a fish hook the first-aider may be justified in doing more than is generally recommended. The instructions above may then be followed. But the first-aider runs the risk of infection developing. Therefore, as soon as feasible, the victim should be examined by a physician. If pain and swelling develop in the injured part in the next few days, if red streaks appear along the limb, or if chills or fever develop, it is imperative to seek medical attention.

FIG. 107 *DEEPLY EMBEDDED FISH HOOK PUSHED THROUGH TO EXPOSE BARB The first-aider simply exerts force at the eyelet of the hook to force the barb up through the skin.*

FOOD POISONING

Definition   Acute reaction of the intestines caused by an irritating substance and characterized by severe abdominal pain, nausea, and weakness. The victim feels a severe griping sensation in the abdomen. Diarrhea, chills, fever, and itching of the skin may occur. Reddish blotches may appear. The hands of the victim may swell.

CAUTION

- Do not give the victim any food, water, or patent medicines prescribed for indigestion.

TREATMENT

1. Have the victim lie down.

2. Induce vomiting by tickling the back of the victim's throat. Place the index finger straight into the mouth and touch the back of the throat gently. This will cause the victim to gag and throw up. Turn victim's head to one side to prevent vomitus from entering lungs. *See page 211, and Figure 101.*

3. Reassure the victim that he will get well.

4. Try to determine the cause of the poisoning, so you can report the facts to a physician.

5. Arrange for medical assistance.

If the victim stops breathing

Apply mouth-to-mouth breathing. *See page 102*.

What the Doctor Says   Food poisoning can be caused by a variety of substances, such as poisonous mushrooms, wood alcohol, or milk which has come from an animal who has eaten a poisonous plant. One's system may be poisoned by an excessive drinking of alcohol, or by an excessive use of irritating spices. Poisoning may also result from the victim's having eaten a fish whose flesh is in itself poisonous.

A common form of food poisoning, known as botulism, results when a victim has eaten canned foods which have not been properly sterilized and in which noxious gases and infectious bacteria have formed. Botulism rarely results from eating commercially canned foods. Although commercial canning methods by and large eliminate this danger, one should be wary of a can that is swollen.

Botulism generally comes from home-canned products which are set up in improperly sterilized or imperfectly sealed jars. This can be suspected if the can is swollen, or, if when the top of a glass jar is removed, a "pop" of gas is noted similar to the opening of a bottle of champagne.

Within 12 to 36 hours, the victim of botulism will sense great fatigue, weakness, headache, dizziness, which will be followed by nausea, vomiting, abdominal discomfort, and diarrhea. If a group of individuals have partaken of the same food, all will develop more or less the same symptoms. In its severe form, botulism can cause paralysis.

Contaminated foods can cause various infections. For treatment, the first-aider is referred to *page 186* on DIARRHEA.

Food poisoning may also derive from an allergic reaction to certain kinds of food. An allergic individual should learn which foods he should avoid by consulting a specialist, who will make such determination through various tests.

In some instances, the irritating substance can be easily determined. For example, the victim may recall that he has eaten some shellfish which he suspected, from the strange odor, were not particularly fresh. On the other hand, the cause of the poisoning may be mysterious.

In either case, there is little that the first-aider can do. The important thing is not to further irritate the intestines by feeding the victim food or water or purgatives. It will be the business of the physician to determine precisely what has caused the trouble, and to deal exactly with the condition. Where, because of vomiting or diarrhea, the loss of fluid is great, it may be necessary for the physician to replace such loss by means of an injection into a vein.

From a medical viewpoint, alcohol is a poison. Limited amounts of the drug can be tolerated by the normal individual; but taken in excess, alcohol will poison the body. Excessive use will bring in its wake all manner of unpleasant symptoms. Some persons are sensitive to even small amounts of alcohol.

The ingestion of toxic substances, such as perfume, hair tonics, etc. which are generally composed of wood alcohol, will cause a severe poisoning. Intense symptoms will develop in a matter of hours. *See page 317* on POISON SWALLOWED.

The eating of berries or shellfish is sometimes attended by acute allergic reaction. In such cases, treatment is to be administered only by a physician.

The eating of poisonous mushrooms generally results in severe symptoms appearing within six hours. In addition to nausea, vomiting and diarrhea, the victim generally experiences an increase of secretion in the eyes and lungs, and wheezing. He feels confused and is highly excitable. However, a victim will generally recover within 24 hours.

The flesh of certain marine animals may cause toxic reactions in man. Even species of fish which ordinarily make good eating may have swallowed another poisonous fish or a poisonous sea plant, and may thus transmit the noxious material to a victim. No easy rule can be established to identify poisonous fish. However, the ingestion of the flesh of such fish is followed by the usual symptoms referred to above, plus the appearance of hives on the skin, headache, nasal congestion, swelling of the tongue, and a difficulty in breathing due to the congestion of the vocal cords. Sometimes a paralytic reaction accompanies this long catalog of untoward reactions, and the victim feels an onset of tingling of the lips, gums, and tongue which gradually turns into a numbness which spreads over the body.

It is generally wise to avoid eating shellfish, eels, or turtles which do not come from a reliable commercial source. However, if one is in a situation where he is compelled to eat fish in order to survive, it is best to cut the fish into small pieces, soak the flesh in fresh or salt water for ten minutes, and repeat the process three times before cooking the fillets in boiling water. The water should then be discarded. If a dog or cat is available, pieces of the questionable fish should be fed to the animal first to make sure that the food is not toxic.

FOREIGN OBJECT IN EAR

CAUTION

- Do not use Q-Tip or any sharp instrument.
- Do not use force.

TREATMENT

1. Using fingers only, the first-aider should remove the foreign body gently.

2. If this cannot be accomplished, call a doctor.

What the Doctor Says   Caution is advised in order to avoid damage to the eardrum which could be serious. If a foreign body is accessible and can be lifted out easily, the first-aider may proceed to remove it. But if it has moved deep into the ear canal and has to be removed with an instrument, it should be done by a physician. The use of a Q-Tip (cotton applicator) may push a foreign body deeper into the canal and may damage the eardrum. Likewise the use of force may injure the ear canal or the eardrum. If in doubt, play safe. Let the doctor do it.

FOREIGN OBJECT IN EYE

CAUTION

- Make sure the victim does not rub his eye.

TREATMENT

1. The first-aider should grasp the eyelash of the upper lid of the victim between his thumb and index finger.

2. Pull the eyelash down gently.

3. Using a wooden matchstick or its equivalent—*see Figure 108*—flip the upper lid back over the matchstick. *See Figure 109.* The eyelid will now stay in that position while the first-aider inspects the eye to locate the foreign body.

4. Use a cotton applicator, such as a Q-Tip, or a piece of cotton on the end of a blunt stick, such as a wooden matchstick or the corner of a clean handkerchief to remove the speck. *See Figure 110.*

If the speck is not readily seen

Search for it on the eyeball with the aid of a bright light.

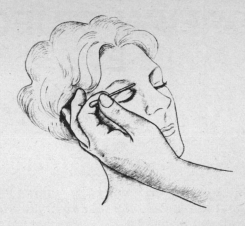

FIG. 108 FLIPPING UPPER LID *To remove foreign body from eye, first-aider must first place a short stick across victim's upper lid.*

FIG. 109 *FLIPPING LID BACK* First-aider grasps upper eyelashes and flips upper lid over stick.

227

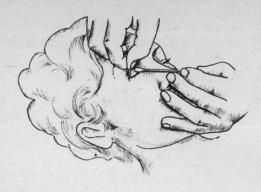

FIG. 110 *REMOVING FOREIGN OBJECT FROM EYE* Holding back the folded-over upper lid, the first-aider removes foreign body with cotton-tipped stick.

If the foreign body cannot be removed easily or cannot be detected

1. Close the eyelid and place a piece of cotton over the eye, or use a sterile eye pad. *See Figure 2, number 12, on page 33.*

2. Keep the cotton in place with Scotch tape or with adhesive.

3. Get the victim immediately to an eye doctor or to a hospital.

If the victim's eyeglasses are broken and glass gets into his eye

1. Have the victim bend over and face the ground.

2. Grasp the eyelashes of his upper lid and gently pull

the lid away from the eyeball, permitting the glass to fall out. Be careful not to rub the eyeball.

3. Get the victim immediately to an eye doctor or to a hospital.

What the Doctor Says At times it will not be possible for the first-aider to remove a small speck of dirt or some fragment in the eye of the victim. This may prove difficult either because the first-aider cannot actually see the offending object, or because the foreign object happens to be embedded in the eye in such a way so that it cannot easily be removed. Evidence that a foreign object remains in the eye will be continued pain, spasm of the eyelids, and a continuous flow of tears. Sometimes these symptoms may be provoked by a minute laceration of the eyeball, an injury so small that the first-aider's unaided eye cannot see the wound.

If such symptoms persist for an hour, it is time for the first-aider to become suspicious, and he should then without further delay get the victim to a physician. Only an ophthalmologist can treat and remove bits of glass or fragments of metal embedded in the eye. Such objects are generally removed by first applying anesthetic to the eyeball so that a proper examination can be made. The physician may also drop a dye into the eyeball which will show up the offending object quite clearly. Modern methods also afford the ophthalmologist an electro-magnet with which he can attract and remove a metal fragment embedded in the eyeball.

FOREIGN OBJECT IN NOSE

CAUTION

- Do not use force.

TREATMENT

1. Remove gently with finger.
2. If not easily removed, call a doctor.

What the Doctor Says A foreign object in the nose is not uncommon among infants or children, who, in play, might sometimes insert a marble or a clip or some other small object into the nose. The main thing is not to panic. Such objects can generally be removed without much ado simply by inserting a finger into the nostril of the victim, or by using a forceps or tweezer.

FOREIGN OBJECT SWALLOWED

TREATMENT

1. If the victim is a child, turn him upside down by holding his legs up. If the victim is an adult, have him bend over a chair, with his head down, to permit object to fall out. *See Figure 111.*

2. Gently tap on the victim's back.

3. Insert a finger in the victim's mouth and sweep your finger across the inside of the mouth to remove the object, if you can possibly get at it. *See Figure 112.*

4. If the object does not fall out, rush the victim to a doctor.

If the victim has difficulty breathing

The object is probably lodged in the windpipe. *See Figure 113 on page 234.* In such a case, apply mouth-to-mouth breathing. *See page 102.*

What the Doctor Says Usually, someone who swallows a foreign object and who feels he is choking becomes panicky. It is important, therefore, to keep reassuring the patient and telling him that you will manage to get the object out of his mouth. Where the object has passed through the mouth and is stuck in the windpipe, summon medical assistance as quickly as possible.

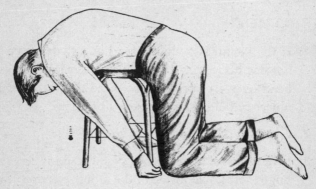

FIG. 111 *REMOVING FOREIGN OBJECT FROM ADULT* *Adult bent over a chair with head down to permit the object to fall out through his mouth.*

Generally, matters of this kind cannot be successfully treated by a first-aider. Sometimes an object goes beyond the windpipe into a large bronchial tube. In such a case, enough air can get into the lungs to allow the patient to breathe. A physician, through X-ray, will be able to study the problem and to remove the object by means of an instrument.

The important decision that the first-aider must make about a foreign body that has entered through the

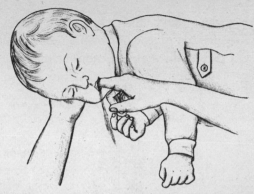

FIG. 112 PUTTING FINGER INTO CHILD'S MOUTH *This child has been held upside down. Presumably the object, lodged in the windpipe, has dropped out into the child's mouth. The first-aider inserts his index finger into the child's mouth to locate and pull out the foreign object.*

mouth is whether or not that object is obstructing breathing. This is a frequent occurrence with children, and if the matter is not handled promptly and handled with understanding, the child can die.

A person beyond middle age who is clutching at his chest may have a foreign body blocking the voice box (larynx) or windpipe (trachea)—or he may be suffering from a heart attack. A rapid way to differentiate the two conditions is to determine whether or not the individual can utter a sound. A victim of even the most severe of heart attacks will be able to utter sounds and speak, whereas an individual with a foreign body stuck in the voice box will not.

233

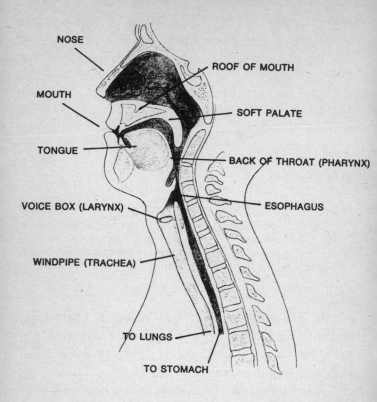

FIG. 113 *CROSS SECTION OF MOUTH, THROAT, WINDPIPE*

In a dire emergency, if the first-aider observes that breathing is fully obstructed—that the victim cannot speak and is beginning to turn blue—an emergency tracheostomy would be justified as a bold attempt to save a life. *See page 115 and Figures 71 and 72.* The first-aider should familiarize himself with this technique.

When turning a patient upside down, sometimes fluid may be emitted from the lungs. This is nothing that should cause alarm. The important thing to remember is that by holding the patient upside down, gravity goes to work and the object is very likely to fall out of the victim's mouth.

FRACTURES AND DISLOCATIONS

Definitions A fracture is a broken bone. There is no difference between a "break" and a "fracture."

In a dislocation, the bone has moved out of its joint.

A fracture-dislocation is a break in the bone plus a dislocation of the bone which have occurred at the same time.

There are two main subdivisions of all fractures:

1. **Closed** (simple). In earlier classifications, this was referred to as a simple fracture. In such injuries there is no open wound in the skin at the site of the fracture.

2. **Open** (compound). An open fracture was formerly classified as a compound fracture. In such a case, the bone is broken and it projects through an opening of the skin. *See Figure 114.* In some instances, the broken bone may only puncture the skin at one small point.

Symptoms The victim suffers severe pain in the region. If the individual moves the region of the fracture or dislocation, or fracture-dislocation, excruciating pain will be experienced. If the region is touched by the first-aider, the patient will experience exquisite local pain.

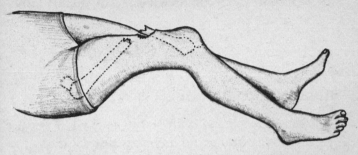

FIG. 114   *OPEN FRACTURE OF LOWER THIRD OF THE THIGH BONE (FEMUR).   Note that the skin is completely broken, and that the bone is projecting out and is exposed to the air. Also note that the thigh is in a deformed position: the victim cannot raise his thigh. The slightest motion would cause severe pain.*

CAUTION

- If the victim has suffered a closed fracture, consider splinting the fractured part before moving the victim. *See pages 80-92.*

IMPORTANT   If the victim is lying in a danger zone, such as an area of fast moving traffic, either:

1. Carefully move the patient to the side of the road to a safe area before any first aid is rendered.

2. Block the traffic flow by parking a vehicle or signaling a detour.

237

TREATMENT OF A CLOSED FRACTURE

1. Splint the broken part. *See pages 80-92.*

2. Transport the victim to a hospital or doctor's office for an X-ray.

TREATMENT OF AN OPEN FRACTURE

1. Cover the wound with sterile gauze. Do not use antibiotic ointment or any antiseptic solution.

2. Apply a roller bandage. *See page 60.* If the application of the roller bandage proves to be too painful for the victim, hold the gauze in place with adhesive tape.

3. Splint the limb as for a closed fracture. *See pages 80-92.*

4. Get patient to a hospital.

FRACTURES AND DISLOCATIONS OF THE UPPER EXTREMITY

Definition The upper extremity includes the fingers, hand, wrist, forearm, elbow, upper arm, shoulder, collar bone, and the shoulder blade. *See Figure 115* showing skeleton of human body.

TREATMENT

In general, first aid of most fractures and dislocations of the upper extremity may be satisfactorily handled by means of a sling, which will give satisfactory first aid pending medical attention. *See page 93.* Certain fractures or dislocations of the upper extremity, particularly those of the wrist and forearm, should be splinted in addition to using a sling. Use a padded wooden splint, *see page 84,* or a pneumatic splint, *see page 89,* or an improvised splint of a folded magazine or newspaper, *see page 81.* If the injury involved is only the upper extremity, and if the victim is conscious and is able to walk or ride, there is no problem in bringing him to a medical facility for further care. If the upper arm (humerus) is fractured, in addition to the sling, the entire upper extremity can be bandaged to the body. *See Figure 59 on page 95.*

FRACTURES AND DISLOCATIONS OF THE LOWER EXTREMITY

Definition The lower extremity includes the ankle, foot, hip, knee, leg, thigh bone and the toe.

TREATMENT

In general, fractures of the lower extremity should be splinted. *See pages 80-92.* However, where a toe is fractured, there is no need to splint. In possible fractures involving the lower extremity, the victim should avoid putting his weight on the fractured part. Carry the victim if necessary, or provide him with crutches, if available. *See page 97.* If no crutches are available, two assistants, one on each side, can assist the victim as external support. *See Figure 62 on page 98.* If only one first-aider is present, have the victim hop on one leg, if he can manage. If available, a walker is easier to use than crutches. *See Figure 61 on page 97.* In cases of fracture involving the lower extremity, it is best to remove the victim's shoes, if possible.

What the Doctor Says An accident may occur in a remote area where medical care cannot be obtained. The first-aider should bear in mind that most fractures and dislocations do not involve problems of severe shock and hemorrhage. There is thus time for careful consideration as to what is the proper cause of action.

In first aid to fractures, it is important to be calm and to reassure the victim. Give the impression that you know what you are doing, that you will render first aid, and that you will readily arrange for expert assistance from a doctor or a hospital.

A good principle to follow is not to move the victim immediately, but to first evaluate the condition. *"Splint them where they lie"* is an excellent principle to follow. A fracture or dislocation of a bone could be relatively simple or may be quite complex and serious. If only a hairline crack in the bone is present and the bone is otherwise intact, the condition might be handled without any repositioning, that is, setting the bone. A cast, a splint, or an adhesive strapping will be sufficient.

An X-ray picture is required to establish for certain whether a fracture actually exists. It is important to obtain X-rays of parts, which to all appearances are only severely bruised or strained, because lurking underneath may, indeed, be a fracture.

A bone may be broken or dislocated or fractured-dislocated, which may cause it to fragment into many pieces, to shatter, to become displaced, to penetrate the skin, etc. The situation requires skillful professional handling and at times, requires an operation by a surgeon. Nonetheless, if a first-aider calmly and correctly follows the directions given in this book, he will render great assistance in relieving pain, preventing further damage to the part, and enabling the victim to be properly transported to a hospital or doctor.

Dislocation, fracture, and fracture-dislocation may present similar symptoms to the first-aider. However, the splinting in all cases is the same.

An open fracture should be treated as a wound. *See page 358.* After the first-aider has covered the part with sterile gauze, and has fixed the gauze in place with a roller bandage or adhesive, he has transformed the injury, for practical first aid purposes, into one that needs the same handling as a closed fracture. Accordingly, after the open wound has been covered, the recommendations for splinting closed fractures should then be followed.

If multiple injuries are present, treat each type of injury separately as if it were the only one involved. Do this in the order of their apparent importance. For example, top priority would be accorded to the control of bleeding. *See page 47.* Next to be managed is traumatic shock. *See page 334.* There may be a combination of injuries such as a closed fracture of the leg associated with a sucking wound of the chest. *See page 162.* In such an instance, treat the chest wound first, before splinting the fractured leg.

There are situations where the first-aider may be in doubt whether or not to splint a part in the region which has been bruised, wrenched, dislocated, or fractured. When in doubt, no harm can be done by splinting. Insist above all that the victim avoid weight bearing. Then let the doctor make the final determination.

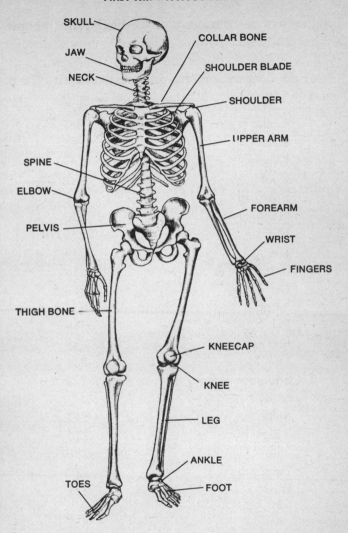

FIG. 115 *BONES OF THE HUMAN BODY*

For first aid treatment of specific injuries, see the following pages:

FRACTURE OF THE COLLAR BONE

TREATMENT

1. Apply a sling. *See page 93.*

2. Seek medical care.

What the Doctor Says   Most fractures of the collar bone can be treated by the doctor with some form of immobilization, either by splint or by bandage or by plaster case. The technique is to wind the bandage around both shoulders in order to hold the fractured collar bone in a satisfactory position. A sling is frequently helpful.

Not uncommonly, a child will develop a greenstick fracture in this location. A greenstick fracture occurs in a soft, flexible young growing bone, one side of which is broken while the other side remains in continuity. This type of fracture is called greenstick because it resembles the break in a green twig in which only one part is actually severed and there is continuity in the other side. Two to six weeks of immobilization is usually sufficient for recovery, depending on the age of the victim and the severity of the fracture.

FRACTURE OF THE ELBOW

TREATMENT

1. Apply a sling. *See page 93.*

2. Seek medical care.

What the Doctor Says Fractures in the region of the elbow require special care because severe swelling may result and affect circulation of the forearm. This could result in permanent interference with wrist movement and finger movement. It is best to get the victim into the hands of a doctor as rapidly as possible.

Sometimes such fractures can be repositioned by a physician without even local anesthesia; but in instances where there is a severe breakage, general anesthesia is required. If the elbow has only been dislocated, then manipulation may be sufficient to put the bones back in place. A doctor should do this.

Where a fracture is combined with a dislocation, an operation may be required. The elbow would likely then be placed into a cast, which can normally be removed in three weeks.

FRACTURE OF THE FINGER

TREATMENT

1. Apply a simple padded splint to the finger. *See page 80 and accompanying figures.*

2. Get the victim to a doctor or a hospital.

If the victim is bleeding from the finger

Treat as you would an open wound. *See page 364.*

What the Doctor Says Generally, a period of somewhere between two to three weeks is required for immobilization of the finger. However, after that period, active motion is desirable.

A crushing, severe injury, such as fingers or a hand caught in a factory machine, is best treated by first controlling the bleeding. *See page 47.* Then apply a sterile dressing. *See page 58.* Then place the victim's hand in a sling. *See page 93.*

FRACTURE OF THE FOOT

CAUTION

- The victim must not bear weight on the affected extremity.

TREATMENT

1. Apply a splint. *See page 80.*

2. Have the victim use external support. *See page 97.*

3. Seek medical care.

What the Doctor Says X-ray determination is required for any severe injury of the foot. Frequently, what appears to the victim to be only a sprain may actually be a fracture. It cannot be emphasized too much that weight bearing should be avoided until the injury has been evaluated by a physician.

An injury may prove to be but a simple crack that can be handled by strapping alone. However, if the bones have been displaced, they will have to be set in place. This can be accomplished, in certain cases, under local anesthesia, but a general anesthesia may be required.

After operating on the fracture, the surgeon will apply a plaster-of-paris cast. About six weeks of immobilization are generally required for healing, but severe fractures may require treatment for twelve weeks or even more.

FRACTURE OF THE FOREARM

TREATMENT

1. Splint the entire forearm and hand. *See page 80.*

2. Apply a sling. *See page 93.*

3. Seek medical care.

What the Doctor Says Fracture of one or two of the bones of the forearm, if the bones are not displaced and are in an acceptable position for healing, will not require setting. In such a case, the application of a plaster cast for six weeks is all that is necessary. However, each case must be individually analyzed as to the necessity for setting, and to determine how long immobilization in the cast is required.

Not infrequently, in an adult, it is necessary to relocate or "set" the broken and displaced bones. At times, this can be accomplished by injecting a numbing medication directly into the fracture site. In other instances, a general anaesthetic is required to relieve pain and muscle spasm. If proper setting cannot be performed, or if the bones slip out of place in the cast after setting, an operation may have to be performed—not to speed the healing, but to maintain the bones in proper position via metal plates, screws, or rods.

Where a child suffers such an injury, an operation is rarely required because future growth will tend to straighten out any deformity present after the bones have healed.

FRACTURE OF THE HAND

TREATMENT

1. Apply a dressing to any open wound. *See page 364.*

2. Apply a sling. *See page 93.*

3. Seek medical assistance.

What the Doctor Says A common type of injury, generally sustained from fist fighting, is a fractured knuckle. Fracture of the hand may also be attended by fracture of the fingers, *see page 247*, or fracture of the wrist, *see page 283*.

If the bone has broken the skin and protrudes, *see page 238* where open fractures are discussed.

A fracture of the hand will usually heal between three and six weeks, depending on its severity.

FRACTURE OF THE HIP

TREATMENT

1. Have the victim lie flat.

2. Transfer the victim to the hospital on a stretcher.

What the Doctor Says If the first-aider suspects a possible fracture of the hip, then the safest thing to do is to have the victim lie down. The victim must not attempt to walk. He should be transferred on a stretcher via ambulance to a hospital. In the absence of a local ambulance facility, and as long as the victim is kept in a horizontal position, no great damage can be done if he is transported in an ordinary autromble, provided the ride is gentle.

Splinting will not be necessary if great caution is taken not to twist the extremity.

At times, a fracture of the pelvis will appear to be a fracture of the hip, and this will not be quite as serious a problem. However, only X-ray examination and evaluation by a physician can authoritatively make this determination.

In general, a fracture of the hip is quite serious. This type of injury usually occurs in older individuals whose bones are somewhat brittle. Operative correction by some form of pinning (internal fixation) or in some instances replacement of the whole head of the thigh bone with an artificial hip (internal hip prosthesis) may be necessary. These modern advanced techniques, developed within the past 25 years, have made it possible for victims to walk again. Previously, such persons would have been permanently invalided and confined to bed or to a wheel chair.

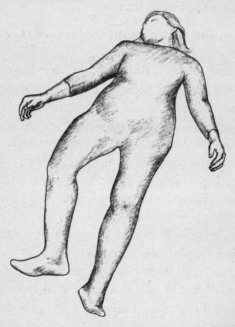

FIG. 116 *SYMPTOMS OF FRACTURE OF THE HIP* *The right lower extremity is shortened and turned out.*

FRACTURE
OF THE JAW

Symptoms A severe pain in the jaw following an accident or a fight. The victim will find it extremely painful to open or close his mouth or to shift his jaw from side to side.

CAUTION

- If the victim is vomiting, do not apply a bandage.

TREATMENT

Apply a circular binding, Barton's bandage, around the jaw and the head. *See Figures 117 and 118.*

What the Doctor Says The objective of the first-aider should be to immobilize the victim's lower jaw by holding that part firmly against the upper row of teeth.

A surgeon will treat a fracture of the jaw by a suitable fixation of the upper and lower teeth. If the victim is treated promptly, the results generally turn out to be good.

FIG. 117 *MAKING A CRAVAT FROM A PIECE OF CLOTH FOR USE AS BARTON'S BANDAGE*
1. *This shows gauze or cloth which has been cut into shape of a triangle (3' x 3' x 4') (93 x 93 x 120 centimeters).*
2. *One corner of triangle is folded up to reach opposite edge.*
3. *Gauze is now folded up once more in half.*

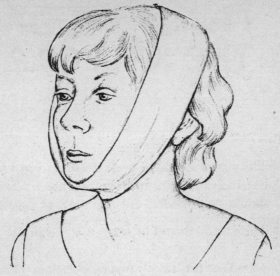

FIG. 118 *SPLINTING A FRACTURED JAW* Tie a cravat around the head and lower jaw. This is known as "Barton's Bandage."

FRACTURE OF THE KNEECAP

TREATMENT

1. The victim should be made to avoid weight bearing. External support, such as crutches or a walker, should be provided. *See Figure 61 on page 97.*

2. The victim should be taken to a hospital.

What the Doctor Says A simple crack in the kneecap may be treated by a physician with excellent result simply by applying a cast. However, if the kneecap has been broken, smashed, or separated, then an operation is required, to be followed by the application of a cast. The results of such an operation are generally good. Prolonged rehabilitation to regain adequate motion of the knee joint and good strength of the thigh muscles is generally required.

FRACTURE OF THE LEG

CAUTION

- Do not permit the victim to bear weight on the extremity.

TREATMENT

1. Splint the fractured part. *See text and figures on page 80.*

2. Have the victim use external support. *See page 97.*

3. Transport victim to a hospital.

What the Doctor Says   Fractures of the leg may be closed or open. If there is an open fracture, dress the wound—*see page 358*—and then splint as for a closed fracture. Depending upon the severity of a fracture, casts are required for six to sixteen weeks, sometimes longer.

During the first six weeks, no weight bearing is permitted. Then the physician may apply a walking cast. This has a heel attachment so that the victim can apply his weight on the ground, and the cast will protect the fracture and allow healing to continue.

Fractures of the leg often present problems of delayed healing, or non-union. Bone graft is then required.

After a major leg fracture, rehabilitation requires many weeks.

Skiers incur many fractures of the leg and ankle. Fortunately, ski patrols around the world are well-trained and efficient. Excellent first aid is usually rendered right on the ski slopes; and the victim is brought promptly to a medical facility for treatment.

FRACTURE
OF THE NECK

CAUTION

- If a fracture of the neck is suspected, do not move the victim.

TREATMENT

1. Have the victim lie flat.

2. Instruct the victim not to bend his neck forward or backward, nor turn his head from side to side. Likewise, the first-aider should make sure not to put the victim's head in motion.

3. The neck should be supported on both sides with pillows, sandbags, or other improvised objects to prevent the victim's head from turning. A flat piece of wood under the head, neck, and shoulders should be used to assure firm support.

4. Transport the victim to a hospital carefully—in a horizontal position, if possible.

If the first-aider is especially trained

He can use the Short Board, *see Figure 3 on page 38,* and an improvised neck collar. *See Figure 119.*

If the victim is able to sit

It may be uncertain whether or not a fracture or dislocation of the neck has been incurred or whether the victim has only suffered a strain of the ligaments. In such a case, a medium-sized Turkish towel or a piece of cloth of equivalent size and thickness should be wrapped around the neck to give the neck firm support. *See Figure 119.* The cloth should not be wrapped so tightly that it obstructs breathing.

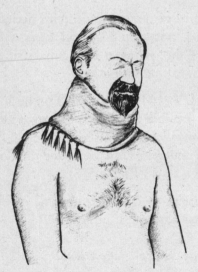

FIG. 119 *SCARF WRAPPED AROUND THE NECK This contrivance will serve as an improvised neck collar and will give support to a possibly fractured neck.*

What the Doctor Says   It is not expected that a first-aider will be able to determine whether or not a fracture or dislocation of the neck has occurred. Very commonly, neck ligaments may only be strained and yet result in severe pain. For example, a person may be sitting in a parked automobile which is struck forcibly from the rear by another vehicle. Within a few minutes to a few days, severe pain in the neck may ensue. In such an instance, wrap the neck in a folded towel to form a broad neck collar.

However, if the injury seems more serious and a fracture or dislocation of the neck is suspected, then follow the instructions set forth above. The short board is mentioned, but its use requires special training gained in a first aid course. Otherwise, any firm surface can be used to form a rigid stretcher, even a sturdy piece of wood. An old door might be used. The main thing is to support the neck, and prevent it from being moved around too much. If no objects are available to form a rigid stretcher, then the next best technique is to wrap the neck in a folded towel.

If the victim has been involved in an automobile accident and he cannot move his arms or legs, or if he has a definite loss of sensation, there may be injury to the spinal cord. In such an instance, he should not be moved. If he is in the line of traffic, cars should be diverted around him until professional first aid assistance can be obtained.

FRACTURE
OF THE PELVIS

Symptoms A fracture of the pelvis may show no gross deformity in the area, but pain will be felt on compressing both sides of the pelvis. *See Figure 120.*

FIG. 120 *TESTING FOR FRACTURE OF THE PELVIS A firm simultaneous compression of both sides of the pelvis should reveal whether the bones have been broken.*

If the bladder has been injured, observe whether or not the urine is bloody. Normal urine is straw colored; bloody urine, pink to dark red.

TREATMENT

1. Have the victim lie flat.

2. Place the victim on a stretcher or on any other firm surface. A long board will do fine. *See Figure 4 on page 38*.

3. Summon an ambulance immediately and transport victim to a hospital.

What the Doctor Says   Generally, a fracture of the pelvis is not a serious condition unless there is involvement of the tube leading out of the bladder. In such case, the victim will pass blood in his urine which will be pink-tinged in color. If this occurs, medical assistance is urgent.

Six weeks of bed rest is usually required for treatment of a fractured pelvis. If the bones are displaced, the doctor may have to use a special pelvic sling to hold the bones in a corrected position while they heal.

Usually, even severe fractures of the pelvis heal without ensuing disability. But some severe types, especially those involving the hip socket, may result in permanent damage. In some instances, extensive deep internal bleeding may result. In certain cases, an operation is necessary to put the bones back in place with metal screws. In a female, though rarely, a markedly displaced fracture may interfere with the pelvic outlet sufficiently to obstruct childbirth.

FRACTURE OF THE RIB

If you suspect a fracture of the rib, press the chest at the site of the fracture. *See Figure 121.* If the victim feels severe pain, the likelihood is that he has sustained a fracture of the rib. Even if no open wound is visible and even if he does not cough up blood, he may, nevertheless, be suffering from a closed fracture.

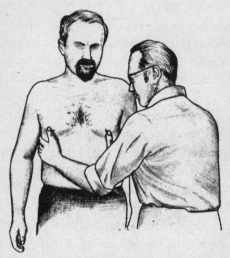

FIG. 121 *COMPRESSION OF BOTH SIDES OF CHEST TO TEST FOR FRACTURED RIB.*

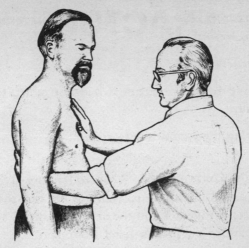

FIG. 122 *COMPRESSION OF FRONT AND BACK OF CHEST TO TEST FOR FRACTURED RIB.*

TREATMENT

Apply a roller bandage or an elastic bandage to the victim's torso. *See Figure 2, number 8, on page 33.* If neither of these is available, adhesive tape can be used, but since tape is generally irritating to the skin, it should be avoided, if possible. Use broad adhesive, two or three inches (5 to 7.5 cms.) wide, and apply firmly halfway around the chest from front to back.

If the victim is a female

Tighten her brassiere by the use of safety pins. This may relieve the discomfort.

If the fracture sustained is an open fracture resulting in a sucking wound of the chest

1. *See text on page 162.*

2. Give the patient one or two aspirin tablets to relieve pain.

3. Bring the victim to a hospital.

What the Doctor Says A closed fracture of the ribs is more painful than serious. Binding the ribs so that the bones come together and the area is rendered immobile should afford the patient relief from pain.

The victim will be more comfortable if he sits up or is propped up in a semi-recumbent position. Lying flat and then getting up from that position may be quite painful, especially during the first week or two.

A canvas rib belt, manufactured in various sizes, helps to support, immobilize, restrict breathing motion, and reduce pain. Such a belt should be worn day and night. For a female victim, a tight wideline brassiere will serve quite as well as a rib belt.

Depending on the severity of the injury or the number of ribs involved, a closed fracture of the rib will require two to six weeks to heal.

FRACTURE OF THE SHOULDER

TREATMENT

1. Apply a sling. *See page 93.*

2. Seek medical care.

What the Doctor Says   Most fractures of the shoulder are successfully treated by binding the injured upper extremity to the body. *See Figure 59 on page 95.* Less injuries may be treated by use of a sling. *See Figure 58 on page 94.* Only on rare occasions is an operation required.

Generally, after such an injury the victim can commence to use his shoulder relatively early, probably within one to three weeks. Such movement is essential to effectually prevent stiffening of the shoulder. Active exercises, under a physician's instructions, are necessary. Full rehabilitation may, however, require many weeks.

FRACTURE OF THE SHOULDER BLADE

TREATMENT

1. Apply a sling. *See page 93.*

2. Seek medical care.

What the Doctor Says For the most part, fractures of the shoulder blade require no more treatment than a sling. Such fractures generally heal satisfactorily. The many muscles in this area help to protect and immobilize the broken bone.

FRACTURE OF THE SKULL

A fracture of the skull can result from a direct blow on the head or from an injury in which the victim either falls to the ground or is thrown to the ground, landing on his

FIG. 123 *OPEN FRACTURE OF THE SKULL*
Victim's head has been split open. Wound goes through the outer skin, and bone is broken so that brain tissue is exposed.

head. A fracture of the skull may also result from a bullet wound or from a blow by a flying object.

A fracture of the skull may be either closed or open. *See page 236.*

It should be kept in mind that a simple laceration of the scalp may bleed profusely and appear to be more serious than in fact it is. In such an instance, the victim is not unconscious, the skull is not fractured, and no brain tissue has been exposed. The first-aider should treat this type of injury just as he would treat any laceration requiring control of bleeding: by the application of firm pressure. *See pages 47 and 364.*

OPEN FRACTURE OF THE SKULL

Symptoms The wound goes clear to the bone and might expose brain tissue. *See Figure 123.* This type of injury should not be confused with a simple laceration of the scalp. *See page 287.* If the fracture is caused by a bullet, the point of entrance in the skull would be small; the point of exit larger. *See page 151.* If the bullet has entered the skull at close range, powder burns may be noted on the skin surrounding the point of entrance.

TREATMENT

1. Keep the victim lying flat.

2. Hold the victim's head back and his chin up in order

to keep his air passages open. *See Figure 63 on page 101.*

3. Cover the wound with sterile gauze or clean cloth. *See page 364.*

4. Bandage the wound with a special head bandage. *See page 74.*

5. Get the victim to a hospital as quickly as you can manage, being careful to keep him lying flat on his back. Avoid a bumpy ride.

If the victim is not breathing

Apply artificial mouth-to-mouth respiration. *See page 102.*

If the pulse is absent and the heart is not beating

See page 99.

CLOSED FRACTURE OF THE SKULL

Symptoms Unconsciousness. Pupils of the eyes are unequal in size. One pupil is open wide while the other is distinctly smaller. *See Figure 69 on page 109.* Bleeding from the ear or the nose may be present. Pulse may be fast, slow, or absent. *See page 42.*

When the victim regains consciousness, he will complain of severe headache, dizziness, and he may indicate that he is seeing double.

TREATMENT

1. Keep the victim lying flat

2. Hold the victim's head back and his chin up in order to keep his air passages open. *See Figure 63 on page 101.*

What the Doctor Says   Skull fractures cannot readily be determined by the first-aider and require X-ray examination. Most skull fractures do not show an open wound. In such cases, the first-aider can and should do nothing.

In a skull fracture, no wound may be visible, not even some bleeding from the scalp. But if the victim recovers promptly from a transient episode of unconsciousness only to lapse into unconsciousness later on, one might suspect internal bleeding around the brain.

In any case, where there is a serious head injury, the victim should be transported with great care and without delay to a hospital. If possible, lay the victim on a stretcher. In any case, avoid a bumpy ride and sudden stops.

FRACTURE
OF THE SPINE

CAUTION

- Be careful not to bend or twist the victim's back. *See Figure 124* on how NOT to carry.

TREATMENT

1. Lay the victim on a firm surface, such as a heavy piece of plywood or an old door. If available, a Long Board will do fine. *See Figure 4 on page 38*.

2. Transport the victim to a hospital.

What the Doctor Says   It is not expected that a first-aider will be able to make a diagnosis of a fracture or dislocation of the spine. In fact, severe strain of the muscles and ligaments of the spine could cause acute and very disabling pain. But treatment should be given if the injury has been more serious than just a simple straining, and if the first-aider *suspects* that a fracture or dislocation may exist. To play it safe, follow the above instruction until medical treatment can be obtained. X-ray examination will enable the physician to make the proper diagnosis and institute the proper treatment.

Many fractures of the spine are not too serious. If the fracture is stable—that is, if there is no displacement of the spine—it is possible to get the victim up and about with the aid of a back brace or corset as soon as the lessening of pain permits. Other fractures or fracture-dislocations—especially if unstable, and this can be determined only by a physician—may require surgical treatment. If the spinal cord or nerves are affected, operation may be necessary.

FIG. 124 *INCORRECT METHOD OF TRANSPORTING A VICTIM Victim may have a fracture of the spine. He should be transported on a solid surface so that any broken bones will be supported and immobilized.*

It is important to make a quick determination as to whether or not the spinal cord or nerve roots have been damaged. Ask the victim to move his toes, feet, ankles, knees, and hips. Test the sensation in the lower extremities by means of a light pinprick, touch, and by the application of heat and cold. If the victim's reactions to these stimuli disclose no departure from the normal, then the spinal cord and the nerve roots have escaped injury.

FRACTURE OF THE THIGH BONE

TREATMENT

1. Have the victim lie flat.

2. Apply a splint. *See page 80.*

3. Transport the victim to a hospital on a stretcher.

If no splint is available

- Strap the affected limb to the normal limb. *See Figure 51 on page 86.*

- Instruct the victim to hold the uninjured limb very rigid.

- Feet, ankles, legs, and thighs should all be tied together by means of a belt, rope, strap, bandage, or cloth.

What the Doctor Says This is a major injury and must be handled with all due respect. At times, a first-aider can be certain that the thigh bone has been fractured if the gross angulation and deformity of the thigh can visibly be noted.

The best kind of splint to use is a *Thomas* splint. *See page 90*. However, this type of splint should only be applied by a trained first-aider. Lacking this particular equipment, the next best thing to use is a padded board which extends from the foot and ankle up alongside the length of the hip. If such a board is applied, the victim can be safely transported to a hospital. He should be kept lying down.

Treatment of this type of fracture can frequently be best accomplished by traction methods in a hospital without the need of an operation; but in many instances, operation by internal fixation with plates, screws, or a rod leading down the marrow may be necessary. Healing of these fractures usually takes from four to six months; in some instances, even longer. This healing process would then be followed by prolonged rehabilitation to gain strength of the muscles and increased range of motion of the knee joint.

FRACTURE
OF THE TOE

TREATMENT

1. Remove shoe.

2. Seek medical care.

What the Doctor Says Very little can be done by way of first aid. Usually, the doctor is able to treat these injuries without the use of casts or splints. Frequently,

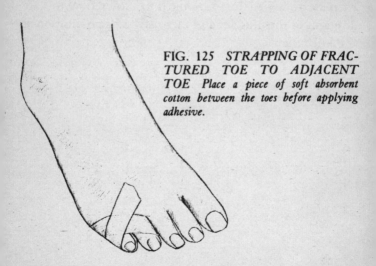

FIG. 125 *STRAPPING OF FRAC-TURED TOE TO ADJACENT TOE Place a piece of soft absorbent cotton between the toes before applying adhesive.*

strapping the injured toe to its neighbor is sufficient to immobilize the injured part and induce healing.

After two or three weeks, the toe should mend. One common type of fracture results from a barefooted individual striking his toe forcibly against a bed or a piece of furniture. Here the fourth and fifth toes are most commonly involved. Though generally the toe will heal in time, activity remains limited for a while by pain and swelling.

FRACTURE OF THE UPPER ARM

TREATMENT

1. Apply a sling. *See page 93.*

2. Seek medical care.

What the Doctor Says   Applying a sling is all that is required of the first-aider. The surgeon generally treats these injuries with a cast or a splint. At times, an operation may be necessary. Healing usually requires six to twelve weeks, followed by many weeks of limbering up for complete rehabilitation.

   If the victim is required to travel a long distance to obtain medical aid, or if he is in very severe pain, the entire extremity in the sling should be bandaged to the body. This will afford more protection, and relief from pain during the jostling of travel.

FRACTURE
OF THE WRIST

TREATMENT

1. Splint the hand, wrist and forearm. *See page 80*.

2. Apply a sling. *See page 93*.

3. Seek medical care.

What the Doctor Says Fractures, dislocations, or fracture-dislocations of the wrist are usually incurred by sustaining a fall on the outstretched hand. Frequently, setting is required followed by the application of a cast. A period of four to six weeks for the wrist to remain in a cast is generally necessary.

At times, a fracture of the small wrist bone known as the *carpal scaphoid* (also known as the *navicular*) will take as long as three to six months to heal, or will not heal at all. This, despite excellent early treatment, will require subsequent operation. Not infrequently, the failure to obtain an X-ray for a severe sprain of the wrist may result in overlooking a fracture of the scaphoid and may be responsible for the failure later to heal properly.

FROSTBITE

Definition Frostbite is the effect of excessive or prolonged cold on the body.

Symptoms The affected part has turned peculiarly white. The victim may experience a tingling in the area, or a special numbness in the area. The victim may feel goose pimples all over his body. His limbs may feel stiffish. The victim may be afflicted by poor judgment, and by an inability to make decisions. In severe cases, the victim may even stop breathing.

CAUTION

- Do not rub or massage the affected part.

- Do not apply excessive heat.

- Do not give the victim alcoholic drinks.

- Do not apply ointments or medication.

- Do not warm the part if the victim must be again exposed to the cold before he can receive full treatment.

TREATMENT

If the victim is outdoors

1. Place the victim's fingers under his armpits.

2. Take off the victim's shoes and wrap his toes in a dry, warm cloth.

3. Cover the victim's nose and ears with a dry, warm cloth. A warm scarf is very effective.

If the victim is indoors

1. Place the victim's fingers and toes in warm water.

2. Apply warm compresses to the victim's nose and ears.

If the victim has ceased to breathe

Apply mouth-to-mouth breathing. *See page 102.*

What the Doctor Says In general, in a case of frostbite, first-aiders tend to be more aggressive in therapy than is good for the victim.

Warm the patient slowly and carefully. Bear in mind that the tissues which have become delicate because of the frostbite may be damaged if handled too roughly. Give the victim warm, nonalcoholic drinks, such as coffee, tea, cocoa, or broth.

If the attack is more than a mild form of frostbite, bring the victim as quickly as possible to a hospital.

Frostbite is an insidious involvement. It does not take place suddenly. The victim may not be aware of what is going on, as it involves the ears, the nose, and the extremities. When exposed to extreme cold, potential victims of frostbite should not adopt an uncomplaining heroic attitude. What is more important than heroics is preventive action. Potential victims should encase the feet and legs in extra wrapping. If one is deep in the woods and there is no chance of reaching shelter, then build a fire. If there is any chance to get to cover, then by all means do so. Prolonged outdoor exposure leads to frostbite.

During World War I, in trench warfare, a condition of frostbite developed among the soldiers which became known as "trench foot." This developed when the victim wore damp or wet shoes which could not be removed for days on end.

In World War II, exposure to cold or icy waters produced "immersion foot." In these cases, the feet developed a bluish color, and there was pronounced numbness. In many instances, gangrene developed. Although the conditions under which "trench foot" and "immersion foot" developed are rare these days, any exposure that leads to dead-looking, bluish, numb feet requires prompt medical attention.

Massaging the affected parts should be avoided. Frostbitten tissues become fragile, and it is possible, by massaging, to rub off sections of skin and produce an open wound which may lead to serious ulceration and infection.

286

HEAD INJURY

IMPORTANT All head injuries must be regarded with the utmost seriousness.

TREATMENT

1. Have the victim lie on a flat surface without a pillow.

2. Transport the victim to a hospital, making sure to move him carefully. Avoid high speed, a bumpy ride, sudden starts and stops.

If there is a laceration of the scalp with profuse bleeding

Apply firm pressure to the wound with sterile gauze or clean cloth. *See page 47* on HOW TO CONTROL BLEEDING.

If the victim is unconscious

1. Lay the victim down.

2. Determine whether or not the victim is breathing. If he is not breathing, *see page 99* on CARDIO-PULMONARY RESUSCITATION.

If the victim remains unconscious

Transport him to a hospital.

If the victim recovers from his unconscious state, has a clear period, followed by another spell of unconsciousness

Transport the victim to a hospital.

What the Doctor Says All head injuries must be regarded with the utmost seriousness until the nature of the injury is evaluated by a physician. There may be a cerebral concussion which, in itself, may not be serious if the victim promptly recovers. For a few seconds following his injury, the victim may be unconscious, and then awake to find himself confused and with a severe loss of memory. The more prolonged the period of unconsciousness, the more likely the serious effects of the head injury. There may be internal bleeding around the brain, and this, indeed, can be a critical matter.

A head injury may be associated with other injuries to the body. For example, there may be a simultaneous injury of the neck. The first-aider should be aware of this possibility, and should examine other parts of the victim's body for possible injury.

If some bone has been fractured, the first-aider should apply treatment for whatever injuries he can handle until such time as the victim can be transported to a hospital. For example, a splint may be applied to a fracture even if the victim is unconscious as the result of an injury to his head.

HEART ATTACK

Symptoms

1. Chest pain, unrelated to any former exertion and becoming increasingly severe.

2. Chest pains feel constricted and remain steady without relief.

3. The pain continues whether the victim breathes deeply or shallowly, or rapidly or slowly. The pain is not influenced by swallowing.

4. The pain is not influenced by a change in the victim's position. It continues unrelentingly whether the victim stands or sits or lies down.

5. The victim exhibits profuse perspiration.

6. The skin becomes pale and cool.

7. The victim suffers from shortness of breath.

8. The victim experiences weakness.

9. The victim may be nauseated, and vomiting may occur.

CAUTION

- Do not give the victim alcohol, food or water.

- Do not apply smelling salts.

TREATMENT

1. Allow the victim to sit, or prop up with two pillows or their equivalent.

2. Summon an ambulance immediately and rush victim to a hospital. If a doctor is near, summon medical aid immediately.

3. If an ambulance is available, transport the victim, sitting up, to a hospital or doctor.

4. If oxygen is available, give to the victim.

If the patient has lost consciousness

Check respiration and pulse. *See page 42.*

If there is no pulse or heartbeat or respiration

Apply cardiopulmonary resuscitation. *See page 99.*

What the Doctor Says Promptness by the first-aider in treatment has saved and can save the life of many a victim of a heart attack. Minutes count—sometimes seconds.

It is terribly frustrating to witness the heart attack of one who is dear to you, for there is truly nothing the first-aider can do beyond the steps outlined above. Do not let this frustration develop into panic, for your panic will communicate itself to the victim of the heart attack. Be composed—that is an essential ingredient in all first-aid procedures, but even more so in the case of heart attack. You can help the victim by doing all in your power to keep him calm until help arrives. Though you may feel the impulse to do more for the victim than the small assistance detailed above, rest assured that you can effectively do no more.

If the victim is past middle age, it is likely that a pain somewhat along the lines described above is indeed a heart attack. Be prepared to apply cardiopulmonary resuscitation if necessary. *See page 99.*

HEAT CRAMPS

Definition Abdominal pain affecting persons who perform labor in an especially hot environment, such as a boiler room, a bakery, or a steel mill.

Symptoms Weakness, dizziness, fatigue, excruciating pain in the region of the abdomen or the lower extremities, excessive sweating.

TREATMENT

1. Give the victim a salt solution consisting of ½ teaspoon of salt in ½ glass of water. Repeat every 15 minutes until the victim feels relief.

2. Apply warm, wet towels to the abdominal region.

What the Doctor Says Heat cramps generally develop in that part of the body which the victim has been using in his work. For example, a laborer in a boiler room who is shoveling coal may feel the cramps in his arms. The cramps generally follow excessive sweating. Where a workman must perform his labor in an excessively high temperature, he should take doses of salt pills regularly so that excessive sweating which he undergoes will not result in cramps. Salt may be ingested in any form, such as salted pretzels or even a slice of bread and butter doused with salt.

Alcoholic drinks, plain cold drinks or stimulants should be avoided. The victim lacks salt and needs salt. The more seriously affected victim may require hospitalization and be fed salt solution through the veins.

HEAT PROSTRATION

Symptoms Enlarged pupils; cold, clammy skin; paleness; weak pulse; shallow breathing; fainting; collapsing.

TREATMENT

1. Transfer the victim to a cool area.

2. Lay him down on his back.

3. Loosen all tight clothing.

4. Apply cool applications to forehead and to the body.

5. Fan him.

6. Make the victim drink a solution of ½ teaspoon salt in ½ glass of cold water every 15 minutes. Three or four doses will be sufficient.

If the victim does not respond favorably within ten minutes

He should be transported promptly to a hospital.

What the Doctor Says Heat prostration, caused by excessive temperature and a loss of body salt, is generally preceded by a feeling of weakness, dizziness, headache, nausea, loss of appetite, and a general feeling of faintness. Transfer to a cool area may then be enough to correct the situation. Prostration itself is not serious, except in an old person or someone feeble from other causes. Injuries may occur if the victim falls to the ground. Alcoholic drinks should be avoided. Plain cold drinks are insufficient. The victim needs salt as well as cold fluids. More seriously affected victims may require hospitalization and salt solution fed through the veins.

HEMORRHOIDAL PAIN

Symptoms Bleeding from the anus, accompanied by acute pain.

TREATMENT

1. Have the victim lie down.

2. Apply an ice bag or an iced wet cloth to the affected parts.

3. Seek medical attention without delay.

If no doctor is available and the painful condition persists

1. Have the victim sit in a warm bath for five to ten minutes.

2. Have the victim lie down.

If bleeding from protruding internal hemorrhoids persists

The first-aider can use clean paper towels or sterile gauze or any clean, soft piece of cloth to gently push the prolapsed hemorrhoids back into the anus.

What the Doctor Says   Hemorrhoids are dilated veins in the anal and in the rectal region. Painful external hemorrhoids or protruding internal hemorrhoids or bleeding internal hemorrhoids are not a serious emergency condition.

External hemorrhoids are usually firm to the touch; internal hemorrhoids are soft. External hemorrhoids are more prone to clot formation, which may be acutely painful. Internal hemorrhoids that prolapse or protrude are likely to bleed. In all these cases, treatment should be obtained from a doctor.

INSULIN SHOCK (OVERDOSE)

Symptoms The victim suffers from hunger and anxiety. He sweats, his heart pounds, and he seems to be in mental confusion. He feels weak and his pulse rate is over 100.

TREATMENT

1. Feed the victim orange juice or any other fruit juice, such as apple, pineapple, grapefruit, canned juice, or a cola drink. If unavailable, feed the victim a solution of sugar water, using two teaspoonfuls or two lumps of sugar to one glass of water. Improvement should appear within five minutes. If no improvement appears, bring victim to a physician or a hospital.

2. If sugar cannot be taken by mouth, use special emergency injectable pack, if available.

If the victim is unconscious

Rush the victim to a hospital or a doctor.

What the Doctor Says Insulin shock is the result of lowered blood sugar. A well-instructed diabetic should be able to avoid insulin shock, or should be able to treat it if it occurs. A known diabetic who has taken an overdose of insulin requires more sugar to repair the chemical balance of his body. A full glass of orange juice or of any other fruit juice will usually correct the imbalance.

A diabetic who develops frequent insulin shock reactions (especially a child who has a severe condition) may be carrying with him a special emergency kit with injectable pack *Glucagon.* If the first-aider is sufficiently trained to perform this injection and he is certain that the treatment is correct, he should proceed with the injection. A diabetic—even a child—should be trained to treat himself, including the injection of medication.

At times, a differential diagnosis has to be made between an overdose of insulin which causes unconsciousness, and diabetic coma which is due to acidosis caused by the diabetes getting out of control. Only a physician is qualified to make such a diagnosis, but the proper approach is to give sugar to the victim and wait five minutes for a favorable response. If there is partial improvement, give another dose of sugar. If there is no improvement, rush the victim to a physician or hospital.

If the victim is in a coma, he should be carrying a health identification card, *see page 28,* or a wrist band or pendant which will lead to prompt diagnosis and treatment.

Special note: Mental confusion may be the dominant sign of insulin shock. There have been instances when law enforcement officers considered the victim to be intoxicated or under the influence of drugs. The victim may be nasty, combative, or resistant to handling. If proper medical care is not administered promptly, permanent brain damage or even death may result.

LIGHTNING STRIKE

Symptoms   Victim is stunned, will fall to the ground, will be rendered unconscious, and will not move, as if dead.

TREATMENT

1. If lightning has struck an individual and no fire has started in the area, it is safe for the first-aider to render care promptly.

2. If a victim appears dead, apply cardiopulmonary resuscitation at once. *See page 99.*

3. If a group of people have been struck, ignore those individuals who show any sign of life and attempt to revive as many as possible of the seemingly dead. As soon as one victim revives, the first-aider should move on to the next. Victims who survive may require repeated pulmonary resuscitation for hours.

4. Transport the victim to a hospital or doctor.

What the Doctor Says   When lightning strikes a person, a very strong electrical current passes through his body and produces the same effect as electrocution. If the current is strong enough, it may cause instantaneous death. But more often, the victim is stunned and only appears dead.

The current affects the nervous system, producing unconsciousness, temporary paralysis of an arm or leg, and cessation of respiration and heartbeat. A victim may seem "foggy" of mind, and may have only limited memory of the preceding events. The victim may also be unable to speak, see, or hear.

Once revived, however, the victim almost always recovers completely within a few hours to a few days. A victim whose heart action has been started may require continued mouth-to-mouth breathing until brought to a hospital. Also, burns and any injuries acquired from falling down may require hospital treatment.

To avoid being struck by lightning during an electrical storm, do not take refuge under a tree; do not go swimming; drop your umbrella, your golf club, or your fishing rod. They may conduct electricity. Do not run. Do not telephone from a booth. Stretch yourself flat on the open ground, ideally on a rubber raincoat or poncho.

If you are indoors, do not stand between an open window and an open door, since lightning seems to follow this pathway.

MISCARRIAGE

Definition   Interruption of a pregnancy by loss of the embryo in the early months (abortion), and the fetus in the later months (miscarriage).

Symptoms   Profuse bleeding from the womb in the early months of pregnancy, occurring spontaneously with no obvious cause. Bleeding may contain blood clots or portions of an embryo. In the later months of pregnancy, the entire fetus may be spontaneously delivered from the womb followed by bleeding.

TREATMENT

1. Apply a sanitary napkin to the victim's vagina, and fix in place by tying to a waist band, front and back.

2. Rush the victim to a hospital. If possible, keep the victim lying on her back.

What the Doctor Says   Continued bleeding indicates that the spontaneous abortion is incomplete. All or part of an embryo or fetus may be identified after it is extruded from the womb. Bring all the extruded material to the physician or hospital. Do not panic. The problem is the same as bleeding alone, and the first aid is the same. Reassure the woman that everything will be all right.

When the patient gets to the hospital, she will be given a general anesthesia. Her womb will be dilated and the fetus will be removed surgically. This is called a *curettage*.

A patient treated in this way will generally recover sufficiently to leave the hospital in a day or two. The convalescence beyond this point will depend on how much blood the woman lost. It may take many weeks for the individual to recover from anemia and regain strength.

When an abortion is attempted by mechanical means, such as using hat pins, needles, wire coat hangers, etc., to dislodge an embryo in the womb, such action may precipitate bleeding and may not cause a spontaneous abortion. It is hardly necessary to point out that any such action is fraught with the greatest danger to the woman, both from loss of blood and from infection of the womb leading to blood poisoning (septicemia), and at times even death.

NOSEBLEED

Treatment refers to a spontaneous nosebleed. Bleeding from local damage to the nose should be treated like any bleeding wound. *See page 364.*

Nosebleed can be very common in normal people and may follow scratching of the nose, infection or a bleeding disease. Occasionally, during menstruation, females will bleed from the nose spontaneously.

TREATMENT

1. Lay the victim flat.

2. Ask him to blow nose gently to expel blood and clot.

3. Gently plug nostril for a distance of about ¾" (2 cms.) with sterile absorbent cotton.

4. Compress both nostrils firmly.

5. Apply an ice cold compress to the nose.

6. If the bleeding is not controlled in ten minutes, consult a physician.

What the Doctor Says Most nosebleeds are simple and originate in the front part of the nose. They are easily controlled by the method outlined above. Bleeding originating from the deeper areas of the nasal cavity require the care of a physician. Blood diseases, e.g. leukemia, hemophilia, polycythemia and purpura, may be the cause of uncontrollable bleeding. If nosebleeds are spontaneous and recurrent, although controlled each time, medical consultation should be obtained.

Old fashioned remedies, such as applying a cold key or cold cutlery or ice to the back of the neck, are not effective. Such measures were intended to induce a spasm of the blood vessels in the nose, and thus control bleeding. However, all that these things can possibly do is divert the victim's attention from what is going on, and perhaps calm him somewhat by making him believe that effective measures are being taken. Despite the possible psychological help, placing cold objects on the back of the neck is not recommended.

POISON INHALED

Definition Noxious air, in the form of gas fumes, smoke, carbon monoxide, tear gas, pesticides, etc., which may be breathed in by the victim.

CAUTION

- Do not give patient alcohol in any form.

TREATMENT

1. Carry the patient—do not let him walk—into fresh air. This must be done without delay.

2. Loosen tight clothing, such as belt and shirt on a man, and brassiere and girdle on a woman.

3. Wrap victim in a blanket to prevent chilling.

4. Keep victim as quiet as possible. Avoid jarring or noise.

5. Summon medical assistance.

If victim has stopped breathing

Apply artificial respiration until experienced personnel arrive on the scene. *See page 99.*

If convulsions occur

Keep victim on a bed in semi-dark room. *See page 181 for special treatment.*

Tear Gas, Blister Gas, Nausea Gas, and Mace

Four types of gases commonly used to control crowds are: (1) tear gas, (2) blister gas, (3) nausea gas, and (4) mace.

There are two types of *tear gas:* CN, a weak gas, whose value is mostly psychological; and CS, a strong gas, which causes coughing, choking, and burning of the skin and eyes. A concentrated dose of CS may cause nausea. *Caution:* The treatment for *mace* is the same as that for tear gas. Use of a wet towel is *not* recommended because the water reacts with the gas on the skin to cause a sensation of severe burning.

To protect the eyes against irritation, put on a pair of air-tight goggles, or a mask of the type used in motorcycling, swimming, and in snorkeling.

To reduce the irritation caused by inhalation of gas, don a surgical mask containing gauze moistened with vinegar. If no mask is available, use a wet handkerchief.

TREATMENT

1. Remove the victim from the gas zone.

2. Have the victim lie down.

3. Douse the victim thoroughly with water.

4. If the eyes are injured, irrigate them thoroughly with water. *See page 202.*

Blister gas is dispensed in a canister as a powder. It is used after a fire hose has been put on a crowd. When the powder comes in contact with the water on the skin, it causes a burning sensation. In fact, blister gas may cause a partial skin-thickness burn. *See page 154.*

TREATMENT

Same as that for tear gas. For a burn caused by blister gas, dry the skin, and apply a thin layer of antibiotic ointment or vaseline, and cover with a gauze dressing and bandage. An alternative technique is to place one layer of vaseline gauze or antiseptic gauze (such as Xeroform or furacin) on the burn. Cover with sterile gauze, and bandage in place.

Nausea Gas causes intense vomiting, instant diarrhea, and possibly rectal bleeding.

TREATMENT

Carry the victim immediately to fresh air. If the vomiting is severe, a physician should be summoned or the victim transported to an emergency facility.

What the Doctor Says   Gas fumes may be the result of

309

carbon monoxide from the exhaust of an automobile, or smoke from a fire, chemical fumes, tear gas, etc. Fresh air contains approximately 80 percent of nitrogen and 20 percent of oxygen. Whatever constitutes the noxious air, the poisons impair the functioning of the human body by depriving it of oxygen. A person cannot survive the complete loss of oxygen for more than four minutes. Some persons succumb in three minutes. If the loss of oxygen is partial, due to inhaling a mixture of air and noxious gases, then the survival time spreads out to a large period.

All fires require oxygen for combustion. When a fire occurs, the victim is deprived of this oxygen.

The reason the first-aider is advised to *carry* the victim to safety and fresh air is that walking in itself uses up oxygen which the deprived body cannot afford. Making the victim lie down while he is recovering from oxygen loss permits a speedier recovery because the victim's oxygen needs are less when he is lying down than when he is standing.

In a case of inhaled poison, artificial respiration, if necessary, should be continued until the victim recovers, or until he is pronounced dead by a doctor. In the absence of a doctor, if a victim exhibits a widely dilated pupil that does not shrink in size when a bright light is focused on it, this can be taken as a sign that recovery is not likely to follow.

Poison inhalation may also occur from overexposure to the ammonia found in refrigerant material. The fluid in a fire-extinguisher contains carbon tetrachloride. When this fluid is sprayed on hot metal, it will form phosgene, a very toxic gas.

Burning plastic will also produce noxious fumes. The effect of any such hot fumes may leave a victim in an apparently satisfactory condition, but a delayed reaction may occur because of the blistering of the lining of the victim's lung. In fact, such a delayed reaction may prove fatal. If the first-aider is in doubt as to the victim's condition, the victim should be hospitalized.

It should be kept in mind that a fire or an explosion may produce multiple injuries such as burns, *see page 154*, wounds, *see page 364*, and fractures, *see page 236*. Confronted by such a situation, the first-aider should handle the most urgent matters first. Only when those are under control, should the first-aider proceed to lesser problems. Apply the principles listed under "First Things First." *See page 22.*

POISON ON THE SKIN

TREATMENT

1. Drench the skin with running water, and keep water running on the skin for ten minutes.

2. Cover the affected part loosely with a bandage or a clean cloth.

3. If patient is in shock, treat as indicated on *page 334*.

4. Keep the victim warm.

5. Summon a physician.

If the victim's clothing is saturated with the poison

Remove such clothing.

What the Doctor Says   Rapid washing and, in some cases, rapid removal of clothing will reduce the extent of poison absorption and minimize the injury.

In treatment, the first-aider should avoid the use of ointments, powders and drugs in any form. Alcoholic beverages should not be administered.

POISON PLANT IRRITATION

It is wise to be able to recognize these annoying plants, so as to avoid contact. *See Figures 126, 127, and 128.*

If the eyes of the victim are involved or if the skin lesions on his body become infected, this may be a serious matter and medical aid should be obtained.

Definition   An irritation of the skin caused by the sap of the stem and leaf of the offending plant.

Symptoms   Within four to fourteen days after exposure, the victim experiences an itching of the skin. Water blisters form on the affected part, gradually increase, and spread over the body. Usually the arms and legs are involved, but the irritation might spread anywhere on the skin and may involve the face, the eyes, and the genitals.

CAUTION

- Victim should not scratch the skin nor rupture the blisters.

TREATMENT

1. Immediately after exposure, wash the exposed parts with hot water and soap.

2. Apply Calomine lotion every two to four hours. Dab the affected parts gently with a clean piece of cloth or a gauze pad. Allow the lotion to dry.

3. If condition is severe and spreading, take the victim to a doctor.

FIG. 126 *LEAVES OF THE POISON OAK*

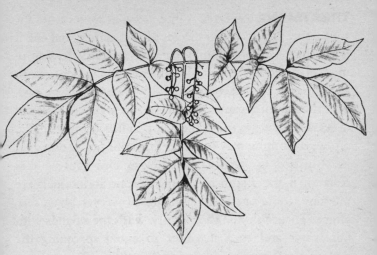

FIG. 127   *LEAVES OF POISON SUMAC*

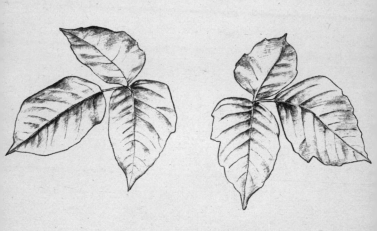

FIG. 128   *LEAVES OF POISON IVY*

315

What the Doctor Says   The sap that oozes from the stem or leaves of certain species of ivy, sumac, and oak is poisonous for some individuals. An allergy to one of these plants indicates that such an individual is sensitive to all of them. The reaction generally becomes worse each time the victim is exposed. The person involved does not necessarily have to touch the plant; indirect contact of the sap with clothing may cause the irritation, and a dog who has brushed up against the sap can also cause a skin reaction if the victim pats him. Certain individuals are immune to the sap of these plants. However, they, too, after exposure should thoroughly wash their hands with hot water and soap in order to avoid spreading the irritation to a person with sensitive skin.

POISON SWALLOWED

IMPORTANT Poisons are divided into two categories—*corrosive poisons,* such as *acid,* and *non-corrosive poisons,* such as *aspirin.* It is important that you quickly determine what the patient has swallowed in order to apply the proper treatment.

CORROSIVE POISONS

ACIDS	LIGHTER FLUID
AMMONIA	LYE
BENZINE	LYSOL
BLEACH	OXALIC ACID
CARBOLIC ACID	PAINT THINNER
CLEANING FLUID	PETROLEUM
DISINFECTANT	SULFURIC ACID
FURNITURE POLISH	TOILET BOWL CLEANSER
IODINE	TURPENTINE

NON-CORROSIVE POISONS

ALCOHOL	HORMONES
ANALGESIC	SLEEPING PILLS
ANACIN	SOAP
ASPIRIN	VITAMINS
BUFFERIN	WAX
EMPIRIN	

If the victim has swallowed a CORROSIVE

CAUTION

- Do not induce vomiting.

TREATMENT

1. If the patient can swallow, make him drink water, milk, fruit juice, or vinegar; or eat raw eggs or mashed potatoes or cornstarch.

2. Call a doctor or an ambulance, or your local Poison Control Center.

If the patient is unconscious

1. Rush the patient to a hospital, or call for an ambulance.

2. Until the ambulance comes, call your local Poison Control Center for instructions.

3. Keep patient lying face down with his head lower than his hips.

If the victim has swallowed a NON-CORROSIVE

CAUTION

- Do not give any food or stimulant.

TREATMENT

1. Try to induce vomiting by placing the blunt end of a spoon at the back of the victim's throat, or tickling the back of his throat with your fingers. You may also induce vomiting by making the patient drink a solution made of two tablespoons full of salt placed in a glass of water. Give one to two cups to a child aged one to five. If the victim is five years or older, make the victim drink as much as four cups. Or give the victim two or three teaspoons of Syrup of Ipecac. *See* FIRST AID KIT on *page 31.*

2. After vomiting begins, place the patient face down with his head lower than his hips to prevent the vomitus from entering the lungs.

3. After the patient vomits, call your local Poison Control Center or a doctor, or rush patient to a hospital.

4. The victim should be made to be still while waiting for transportation.

What the Doctor Says   Children between the ages of one and five are common victims of household poisoning. Swallowing aspirin accounts for 25% of the incidence of poison cases in children under the age of five.

In a house where there is a child under five, all medicines and most household substances, such as petroleum derivatives, lye, and cleaning solutions, should be kept under lock and key. Keeping poisoning agents in a closed closet is not sufficient protection against the ever-present danger that the prying child will open the closet and drink or eat lethal poison. Parents would do well to avail themselves of "childproof" containers which are available today.

Alcoholic beverages, acids, and a number of other common products may cause death to children, and should be kept out of their reach.

In cases of attempted suicide, an adult commonly takes an overdose of sleeping pills; and where it is known that some person in the household is melancholy or suicidally directed, every attempt should be made to keep such substances out of reach. *See page 191.*

Severe poisoning may be caused by the ingestion of insecticides, pesticides, acids, and such alkalis as lye, benzine, turpentine, paint thinner, lighter fluid.

Poisoning can also be caused by the ingestion of certain species of mushrooms or by eating poisonous fish or shellfish which have decomposed.

When taking the victim to the hospital, it is important for the first-aider to make sure that he puts the substance responsible for the poisoning in a container and brings that container to the hospital. *If no poison is available, collect some of the vomitus and bring the specimen to the doctor.* Analysis will help the physician decide on the best treatment.

If the patient is unconscious, is experiencing a convulsion, or has a severe burning sensation in the mouth or throat, do not attempt to induce vomiting. The burning substance is at work and is doing terrible damage. The best thing to do is to neutralize the force of the poison. Therefore, give the patient milk, if available, or if not, water, fruit juice, or vinegar. Raw eggs, mashed potatoes or cornstarch will lessen the strength of the poison.

As many as two million American children accidentally ingest toxic materials in a single year, and approximately 500 tots die as a result. With care, these deaths could be avoided. Substances such as medicines cause one-half of the child poisonings—only one-half. It may be surprising that household products cause the other half. Children between 18 months and two years suffer most poisoning accidents. A child of this age is irrepressibly curious, and will open up any can or jar in sight and satisfy his curiosity to the fullest by eating or drinking the substance. Parents should realize that all cleaning fluids are potential agents of death. Every care should be taken to keep these out of the hands of the young toddler.

The United States Government maintains approximately 550 Poison Control Centers throughout the country. It is a wise precaution to find out the phone number and the location of your local Poison Control Center and to write this on a piece of paper and paste the paper on the inside of your medicine chest. Looking up the phone number and finding the address after poison has been taken may consume too much time. When calling a Poison Control Center, give your name, address, and phone number, and try to identify in as few words as possible the substance that was taken. The Control Center may be able to give valuable advice and send a physician and an ambulance.

PREGNANCY CONVULSIONS

Symptoms   Headache, drowsiness, a feeling of depression, restlessness, confusion, a blurring of vision, nausea and vomiting will generally precede a pregnancy convulsion. This is a serious condition which requires immediate medical aid.

TREATMENT

1. For first aid treatment, *see* EPILEPSY on *page 199.*

2. Summon an obstetrical specialist.

3. Arrange for immediate hospital care.

What the Doctor Says   Toxemia of pregnancy is an abnormal state in which the woman is unable to adapt to the pregnant condition.

Careful medical attention will detect this condition in an early phase, and severe complications can be avoided. Neglected or uncontrollable toxemia of pregnancy may lead to convulsions. Convulsions in pregnancy will not occur unless symptoms listed above have been present for at least several hours.

PSYCHIATRIC DISTURBANCE

Definition An individual may be markedly depressed, talk of suicide, be excited, hyperactive, yell, do a lot of talking that does not make sense, be threatening and potentially violent, hear voices, etc.

GENERAL GUIDELINES

1. A disturbed and excited victim is usually terrified and panic stricken. Action by the first-aider may be misinterpreted as a further threat.

2. The victim is very often lacking in self-respect. Accordingly, he will be hypersensitive to any intervention that seems to reduce his sense of self-esteem.

3. You are not required to precisely diagnose the victim's condition. It is sufficient if you realize that the victim exhibits significant mental disturbance.

4. Do not treat the victim in a patronizing manner.

5. Do not argue with the victim.

6. Do not order the victim about; do not use harsh or threatening language.

7. Do not restrain or touch the body of the victim unless there is danger of self-damage or injury to some other person.

8. Be patient. Talk in a quiet, confident voice; be kind and reassuring.

9. Engage in conversation. Listen for clues of what is causing the disturbance. Try to divert the victim from harmful acts.

10. No matter what the victim says to you, do not take the remarks personally. Remain calm, and treat the victim with respect.

11. Do not try to solve the problem alone. Contact a relative, a physician, or a policeman, and call an ambulance. A relative, known to the victim and calling the victim by his first name, may be helpful, indeed. At times, a relative may furnish valuable information that may be helpful in managing the victim. Only one relative should be allowed to speak to the victim. More than one person talking to the victim at any one time may generate confusion.

12. If the first-aider is afraid of the victim, he should not engage in any conversation until he is sup-

ported by the helpful presence of an officer of the law or by someone who will be able to handle the victim, should he become violent.

Guidelines for Suicidal Behavior

1. Do not underestimate the danger of suicide by assuming that the victim is bluffing. Consider seriously any threat of suicide. *It is not correct that a person who talks of suicide will not complete the act.* Threats of suicide may precede the fatal act by weeks. Sleeplessness, loss of weight, and early morning agitation—all symptoms of depression—may precede a suicide attempt.

2. A victim of depression, recently discharged from a hospital, even if he is improving, may encounter serious difficulty in adjusting to the world outside the hospital. Such a victim may commit suicide.

3. Encourage the victim to talk about his suicide plans. Try to understand the victim. Be sympathetic.

4. Arrange for psychiatric care.

Guidelines for Manic Behavior

1. Even the "jolliest" manic patient has a core of

sadness lurking inside himself. He may be overly happy, may talk loud, fast, and excessively.

2. Though he may be quite funny, do not participate in his "fun."

3. Speak calmly and seriously. State in unmistakable terms that he needs the help of a doctor.

4. Arrange for psychiatric care.

Guidelines for Recognition of Schizophrenic Behavior

1. The victim may hear "voices" speaking to him, or he may "see" things (hallucinations).

2. The victim may think he or she is someone else— like Napoleon, or Moses, or the Virgin Mary (delusions).

3. Keep in mind that there still remains a sensible inner core inside the most insane victim. Address yourself to that sensible area. Approach the victim as if he is in the grip of a nightmare. Act calm. Try to be reassuring.

4. Assume that the victim is listening to you. Attempt to make him more trusting and cooperative, even though he appears inattentive.

5. Your job is to get him to agree to medical assistance. Arrange for psychiatric care.

What the Doctor Says   The most important thing to keep in mind is that you are rendering first aid. Do not attempt to diagnose the disorder or render psychiatric care. That is a job for a professional.

Try to control the situation by following the guidelines set forth above.

Also, bear in mind that conditions other than a psychiatric disturbance may cause abnormal behavior. Particularly deceptive at times may be the odor of alcohol on the victim's breath: this may lead to an erroneous judgment that alcoholic intoxication is the cause of the mental disturbance, when in fact, an underlying condition of insulin shock, or brain tumor, or drug overdose, or head injury, or infection, may be the causative force of the disturbance.

A victim suffering from insulin shock *(see page 298)* may be nasty, combative, and confused, until sugar in some form is ingested. A brain tumor may cause a severe headache, or some wild and destructive behavior. Some individuals react very poorly to small amounts of an alcoholic beverage, much less than is generally required to cause intoxication (pathological intoxication). Such a person may become wild, destructive, and uncontrollable.

An overdose of drugs in an individual who is not an addict may cause abnormal behavior. Peculiar behavior may follow a head injury *(see page 287)*. A virus or some other infection affecting the brain and its coverings (encephalitis or meningitis) may cause a psychiatric disturbance. Talking to the victim or to someone else on the scene may afford a clue as to the cause of the trouble, and may help in first-aid management.

In the case of mental disturbance, the role of the first-aider is quite limited. The victim should be brought under professional care as soon as possible.

PUNCTURE WOUNDS

Note *See page 364 for general treatment of wounds.*

TREATMENT

1. Wash the affected part thoroughly with white soap or antiseptic soap and water.

2. If possible, squeeze out blood from the wound.

3. Apply a clean—or preferably, sterile—dressing.

4. Keep weight off the affected part—especially the foot—if possible.

What the Doctor Says   The general principles of first aid for wounds and lacerations apply. *See page 364.* The special danger created by a puncture, such as stepping on a rusty nail, is that a serious, deep infection may develop—so-called lockjaw, or tetanus. Lockjaw is not a medical term but refers to the severe generalized spasm of muscles that afflicts the victim. This condition leads to death.

The tetanus bacillus will grow without oxygen, and hence is referred to as an anaerobic organism. A perforating wound such as that caused by a nail does not allow oxygen to reach its depths and thus encourages the growth of an anaerobic organism. A physician will determine the necessity for tetanus anti-toxin or the use of some antibiotic such as penicillin.

If the victim is somewhat isolated from medical care and the first-aider observes the development of all or some of the following symptoms, the need for medical attention is urgent:

1. Increasing pain.

2. Increasing warmth.

3. Increasing redness.

4. Increasing throbbing of the wound.

5. Tender nodules swelling in the groin.

RADIATION EXPOSURE

CAUTION

- The first-aider should not venture into an area of radiation without the supervision of a Radiation Safety Officer of the Nuclear Regulatory Commission or any other expert. Radioactive energy is invisible; it emits no sound; it produces no special sensation. Familiarity with the Universal Radiation Symbol is important. *See Figure 129.* All containers, vehicles, installations, or storage areas for radioactive materials are marked with this symbol.

What the Doctor Says If the first-aider observes an accident such as an explosion, fire, spillage, or collision and notes the Universal Radiation Symbol, he should not venture into the area until he has contacted the Nuclear Regulatory Commission or received guidance from an expert. State Police will help contact the proper individual. A Radiation Safety Officer, by means of a radiation detection instrument, will determine the presence or absence of radioactivity and the level of the destructive gamma rays. The Radiation Officer or other expert will decide if the area can be entered and for what length of time.

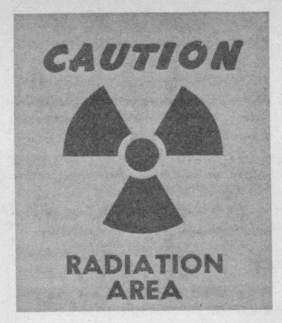

FIG. 129 *UNIVERSAL RADIATION SYMBOL*

It is apparent that the role of a would-be first-aider is sharply limited because of the presence of radiation. Victims contaminated with radioactive materials must be processed through a decontamination center. While burns and blast injuries may require first-aid treatment, the effects of the radiation itself are not usually amenable to first aid other than decontamination. These effects take days or weeks to show themselves unless the exposure is massive; in that case, vomiting and other symptoms may be immediate.

333

SHOCK

Symptoms   The victim turns pale, becomes cold, and his skin gets a clammy feeling. He has a vacant look in his eyes, with lack-luster, dilated pupils. He appears to be breathing in a shallow manner, irregularly and rapidly. The pulse is fast and weak. The victim experiences a general feeling of weakness and a pronounced thirst. There is a fall in his blood pressure, and his answers to questions are sluggish. The victim is restless.

CAUTION

- If the victim is conscious and you know that medical aid can be obtained within 30 minutes, do not give him water to drink.

- Do not give the victim any alcoholic beverage.

If the victim is unconscious or nauseated

Do not give him water.

TREATMENT

1. Loosen tight clothing, particularly around the neck.

2. Have the victim lie down flat. Elevate the feet. *See Figure 104 on page 212.*

3. Keep the victim warm. Cover his body with a blanket or an overcoat.

4. Promptly transport the victim to a hospital.

If the victim is bleeding profusely

Apply pressure. *See text on page 47 relative to control of bleeding.*

If the victim has difficulty in breathing

He will need oxygen. Transport the victim to a hospital as soon as possible.

If the victim has suffered a head injury

See HEAD INJURY on *page 287.*

If the victim is not breathing

Apply mouth-to-mouth breathing. *See text on page 102.*

What the Doctor Says In shock, the blood volume is reduced, as fluid shifts out of the blood into the tissues. This induces an abnormal condition in which the heart is unable to pump sufficient blood throughout the body. The nutrition of the tissues suffers because of oxygen lack, and such lack is critical. If shock is not promptly counteracted, the victim's heart will get weaker and begin to fail.

The victim may appear hale and hearty, but in the very next moment, suddenly collapse. As soon as the first-aider observes signs of shock, he should proceed without delay to administer the recommended treatment. Rapid, correct application of first aid may save a life. Continue the treatment while transporting the victim to a hospital.

SHOCK FROM MARINE ANIMAL

Definition   Electric shock caused by the electric eel or the catfish which inhabit fresh waters, or by the stargazer or the ray which inhabit salt waters.

Symptoms   The victim feels somewhat stunned, either in the part that has been shocked or over his entire body. He may feel paralyzed.

TREATMENT

Assure the victim that the situation is not dangerous and that no permanent injury will result. The paralysis is not a true paralysis. No specific treatment is necessary.

What the Doctor Says   It is very rare for the electric shock from a marine animal to prove fatal. After a period of reaction to the shock, the victim generally recovers after 10 to 30 minutes.

SKIN SCRAPED (ABRASION)

CAUTION

- Do not apply tincture of iodine, which is too strong to be used.

- Other antiseptic solutions which contain alcohol may cause uncomfortable burning and are quite unnecessary.

TREATMENT

1. Shave the area, and the surrounding zone.

2. Wash the wound thoroughly with soap and water. Use sterile cotton balls if available. If unavailable, use any clean cloth. Use plain white soap or an antiseptic bar soap, such as *Dial,* or liquid antiseptic soap, such as *Physohex* or *Septisol* or *Betadyne.*

3. Dry the area.

4. Apply an antibiotic ointment, such as *Bacimycin* or *Neosporin,* to the abrasion. Use a Telfa* dressing or a

*The trade name used by The Curity Company for non-adherent dressing is TELFA.

band-aid. If neither is available, the first-aider can apply a gauze dressing. If no gauze is available, use any clean piece of cloth.

5. Tie the dressing in place with a roller bandage.

6. Hold the roller bandage in place with adhesive tape. If no adhesive tape is available, tie up the bandage by using the roller bandage itself. *See page 60.*

What the Doctor Says For the general abrasion, a treatment of plain soap and water and an antibiotic ointment will well serve the purpose. However, an iodized soap, such as *Betadyne,* or a Hexochlorophene soap (*Physohex* or *Dial* or *Septisol*) are recommended.

Once the initial treatment has been rendered, and early healing without infection has begun, discontinue the use of ointment because it keeps the abrasion moist and macerated. Shift to simple dry dressings. An antiseptic powder should be used to help dry the abrasion and encourage the formation of a scab.

For further information, *see* BRUISE on *page 149,* WOUNDS AND LACERATIONS on *page 364,* PUNCTURE WOUNDS, on *page 330.*

SPLINTER

TREATMENT

1. Grasp the splinter between your index finger and your thumb. If the splinter is not projecting far enough out of the skin so that it can be grasped with the fingers, use a tweezer.

2. Pull out the splinter, bearing in mind that this operation requires withdrawal at the same angle that the splinter entered the skin.

3. After removal, wash the area thoroughly with soap and water.

4. Apply a band-aid. *See page 58.*

If the splinter is deeply embedded

1. Remove the overlying skin by taking the following steps:

    a. Sterilize a needle by either immersing it in alcohol, or by heating the tip of the needle in the flame of a match.

    b. With the sterilized needle, remove the outer layer of skin by piercing it layer-by-layer until the end of the splinter is uncovered.

If the splinter cannot be removed

Take the victim to a hospital.

What the Doctor Says Splinters of wood or thorns are usually embedded in the skin at an oblique angle. They may penetrate only the outer layers of the skin, or may extend deeper into the subcutaneous tissue below the skin. It is those splinters that are deeply embedded that cause trouble and resist removal.

The first-aider should limit himself to the procedures described above. If the object still cannot be removed, he should seek medical assistance.

SPORTS INJURIES

With many more millions of people, old and young alike, indulging in various sports, athletic injuries are becoming ever more numerous. By following the instructions for handling injuries found throughout this book—various fractures, sprains, bruises, etc.—the first-aider will be able to manage most sports injuries which require on-the-spot treatment.

Particular sports tend to produce specific types of injury. For example, ice skating is likely to cause a fractured wrist, whereas skiing will generally result in fractures of the ankle and the leg. American football takes its toll of knee injuries—especially ruptured knee ligaments—while tennis is more likely to produce a ruptured muscle in the calf. Injuries common to boxing are fracture of the nose or the jaw, brain concussion, and lacerations about the eye.

CAUTION

- An injured player should be removed from the game until the nature and extent of the damage has been carefully assessed. The former habit of heroic denial of pain and continued play is foolhardy and dangerous.

STINGS
OF INSECTS

The insects that sting are the: hornet, yellowjack, honeybee, wasp, scorpion, tarantula, black widow spider, brown recluse, ant, tick, blister beetle, and puss caterpillar.

CAUTION

- The most serious problem that may result from the sting of an insect is a rapidly developing and severe generalized reaction. Infants and young children are particularly susceptible. Such a reaction is usually signaled by intense pain and swelling of the region; nausea and vomiting; dizziness; tight muscles; sweating; difficult breathing; the appearance on the skin of raised, irregular shaped, reddish blotches which itch; convulsions; coma. Any of these signs may indicate serious trouble.

EMERGENCY TREATMENT

1. If the bite is on an extremity, apply a venous tourniquet immediately. *See page 51.*

2. Apply an ice-cold compress to the area of the bite.

3. Emergency tracheostomy may be required, if the swelling of the voice box (larynx) obstructs breathing. *See page 115.*

4. Seek medical help promptly.

What the Doctor Says Fortunately, it is quite rare for death to result from an insect bite. Even in severe reactions, there is usually sufficient time in which to obtain assistance. Most often, local pain and a general sick feeling throughout the body will be experienced. Once it is apparent that the victim's reaction is more than local, a venous tourniquet is indicated. *See page 51.*

Of all the stinging insects, the brown recluse is perhaps the most dangerous. The reaction to a brown recluse sting is somewhat similar to that of snake bite: local irritation spreads and there is some death of local tissue. The best treatment for such a reaction is to incise (cut) the area just as in snake bite. *See page 139.* This should be done by a physician; but if the victim is in a remote area and no medical care is available, a bold, well-trained first-aider might be forced to take this drastic action.

If, after a bee sting, the black stinging apparatus is still in the skin, it should be carefully removed with a tweezer, since its continued presence allows more of the toxic material to enter the body. Generalized allergic reactions to bee stings tend to get worse with successive stings. Such victims should be desensitized by medical treatment.

The bite of the feared black widow spider is rarely fatal except to infants and very young children. Severe abdominal pain may result, mimicking acute appendicitis. Severe muscle spasm will be relieved by the injection of calcium gluconate by a physician.

The tarantula sometimes accompanies a shipment of bananas, and strikes an unsuspecting person on the loading docks. This bite will cause intense pain and a local wound, but is not likely to cause a generalized reaction. The bite is not fatal.

Once in the hands of a physician, a victim with a generalized reaction may require the administration of epinephrine injections and/or antihistaminics and cortisone.

Ticks bury themselves in the skin. Treat the sting by covering the area with any kind of oil to suffocate the creature. Within thirty minutes, the tick can be lifted out. Then wash the area thoroughly with soap and water. Ticks may transmit Rocky Mountain spotted fever, an ailment not confined to the Western part of the United States. A physician should be consulted, since antibiotic therapy may be indicated.

When trying to remove a troublesome bee hive, be sure to be well clothed with protective gear, including a special hood.

An episode of multiple stings of any of the above insects increases the danger of severe toxic reaction and even death.

STINGS OF MARINE ANIMALS

Definition Stings caused by the jellyfish, the Portuguese man-of-war, the sea nettle, the sea urchin, the stingray, the octopus, the squid and certain sea snakes. *See Figure 130, Figure 131, and Figure 132.*

Symptoms The victim suffers severe local pain accompanied by a paralytic sensation. He may experience shock.

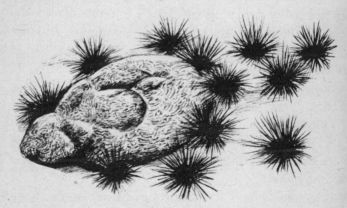

FIG. 130 *SEA URCHINS AROUND A ROCK Note the black color of the sea urchins and the sharp spiny projections emerging from their bodies. These spines contain barbs which are difficult to withdraw.*

TREATMENT

1. Give the victim a dose of morphine. If morphine is not available, administer any strong pain-relieving drug. If no drug is available, give the victim two pills, 10 grains (600 milligrams), of aspirin every three hours.

2. Apply a tourniquet between the place of the sting and the heart. *See text on page 51 and accompanying figures.* Tighten sufficiently for the veins to bulge out somewhat. Release the tourniquet for one to two minutes out of each 15 minutes, then re-apply. Repeat this cycle 10 times.

3. Immerse the affected arm or the affected leg in ice water from five to ten minutes.

4. Get the victim to a hospital.

If the victim experiences shock

Apply treatment set forth on *page 334.*

If barbs of the sea urchin have entered the victim's skin

See page 340 on removal of splinters.

What the Doctor Says Persons swimming or frolicking in waters which abound with creatures which sting should learn the habits of such marine animals and learn how to avoid contact with them.

When a person has been stung by a marine animal, the problem is not one primarily of controlling the bleeding. Therefore, the tourniquet need not be tightened as much as it should be in arterial bleeding; it is sufficient that the veins be engorged.

Unlike treatment for a snake bite, incision of the affected area followed by suction of the wound is not recommended.

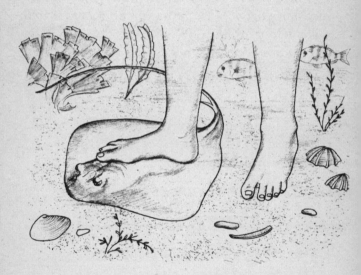

FIG. 131 *VICTIM STEPPING ON STINGRAY* Damage is done by tail of stingray.

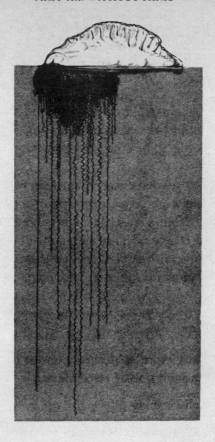

FIG. 132 *PORTUGUESE MAN-OF-WAR ON SURFACE OF WATER* *This animal has long tentacles. If a swimmer comes in contact with these tentacles he will experience a sting.*

STROKE

Definition   An interruption of the blood supply to the brain resulting in reduced brain function. Stroke is also known as apoplexy, or cerebrovascular accident.

Symptoms   A sudden onset, frequently without warning, of bulging neck veins, drooling of the saliva. The victim's face becomes red and congested; the mouth may gradually pull to one side; the victim may find it difficult to speak. The victim may suddenly collapse and fall to the ground; vomiting may occur; and coma may rapidly develop.

TREATMENT

1. Have the victim lie down. Elevate his head and shoulders with one or two pillows.

2. Loosen all clothing.

3. Apply cool compresses to his forehead.

4. Transport to a hospital. (Keep in lying down position).

If vomiting occurs

See page 211.

If convulsions occur

See page 181.

What the Doctor Says   A stroke or cerebrovascular accident may result from either brain hemorrhage, the clotting of an artery in the brain, or an artery leading to the brain, or from an embolism. An embolism is a clot breaking off at another part of the body and moving to the brain. Although in many cases a physician may be powerless to influence the outcome, in certain instances specific corrective treatment may be possible.

For example, a large artery in the neck (the carotid) may be blocked, diminishing blood flow to the brain. It is possible to detect such a blockage by an X-ray (arteriogram) of the blood vessels after injection of a dye. Through surgical procedure, the artery can be unplugged, and the patient can then be placed on drugs which prevent blood clotting (anti-coagulants). Complete recovery is possible.

Unfortunately, in the event of a stroke, there is little for a first-aider to do beyond arranging for proper medical attention.

SUNBURN

Definition An irritation of the skin caused by overexposure to sunlight.

Symptoms The skin becomes red and swells. The victim experiences pain. In more severe cases, there may be blister formation, headache and fever.

TREATMENT

1. Carry the victim to a cool place.

2. Apply ice cold compresses, wetted with one part of milk mixed with four parts of water, to the affected parts. Apply these compresses for 10 minutes out of every two hours until adequate relief is obtained.

If there are severe blisters, severe headache, or fever above 101 degrees

Seek medical assistance

If the victim experiences severe pain

Give the adult victim two aspirin tablets every four hours. If the victim is a child, reduce the dosage to one aspirin tablet. If aspirin does not effectively reduce the pain, give the adult victim one 65 milligram darvon tablet every four hours. If the victim is a child, reduce dosage to one 32 milligram darvon every four hours.

What the Doctor Says   A skin not previously exposed to sunshine is more susceptible to sunburn than a surface that has already been tanned. Skin sensitivity varies with each individual. A light colored skin is more likely to burn on slight exposure than a darker skin. The darker the pigment of the skin, the less sensitive it is to sunlight.

Sunburn can afflict a victim even on cloudy days, since the ultraviolet rays of the sun, responsible for the burn, penetrate the clouds. Even if a person remains shielded from the direct rays of the sun, reflection of the sun's rays from snow or from the waters of a lake can cause sunburn. Excessive exposure to rays of an ultraviolet lamp can also cause a severe skin burn.

Commercial suntan lotions afford only partial protection. Persons with sensitive skin should avoid excessive exposure.

SUNSTROKE (HEAT STROKE)

Symptoms The victim experiences headache, dizziness, abdominal discomfort, decreased sweating, feels faint. His skin becomes dry, hot, and red. There may also be delirium, unconsciousness, a pulse which rises above 110 per minute, and rapid breathing, 30-40 times per minute. The body temperature is greatly elevated, often to 103 degrees, and may run as high as 106 degrees.

TREATMENT

1. Transfer the victim to a cool area.

2. Lay the victim on his back.

3. Loosen all tight clothing.

4. Apply cool applications to his forehead and to his body. Sponge the body with *tepid* water. If available, use equal parts of rubbing alcohol with water.

5. Fan the victim.

6. Get the victim to drink a solution of one-half teaspoon salt in one-half glass of water every 15 minutes. Three or four doses should be sufficient.

7. Massage the arms, and the feet, and the legs. Work all movements towards the heart.

8. Rush victim to a hospital.

What the Doctor Says Sunstroke, known medically as *Heat Pyrexia,* often afflicts older people and alcoholics on very hot days. The victim does not necessarily have to be exposed to the sun. The attack can result from a hot, humid environment even if the victim is indoors. The effect is that the body's regulatory heat mechanism is blocked. Sweating ceases, and there is an interference with the normal loss of body heat.

Artificial means of enabling the victim's body heat to escape must be adopted. If sponging the victim with tepid water does not effectively reduce his temperature, the victim should be plunged into an ice water bath until his temperature goes down to at least 103 degrees, and the pulse rate lowers to 110 per minute. Generally, treatment of sunstroke is successful, and the victim recovers without untoward effect.

TOOTHACHE

Definition   A pain caused by a cavity or abscess in a tooth.

TREATMENT

If an open cavity in the tooth is obviously the cause of the toothache

1. Clean out the food particles from the cavity with a toothpick.

2. Then pack the cavity with a very small piece of cotton soaked in oil of cloves.

If the toothache derives from a cause not readily visible

The ache may be caused by an abscess in the root of the tooth or by some other irritation. Seek dental aid without delay.

What the Doctor Says   There is nothing quite so harrowing as an incessant, throbbing toothache. If it is at all possible to get the patient to a dentist or a hospital clinic, then do so. However, if the toothache occurs when the victim is far away from a dentist or a hospital, and no medical aid is obtainable, then use treatment prescribed above. If oil of cloves is not available, then some form of sedation should be administered for the pain. A pain-relieving drug, such as aspirin, darvon, etc., should be administered. For more severe pain, narcotics prescribed by a physician, such as codeine or other opiates, may be necessary. Before venturing into an area without dental facilities, it would be advisable to have the teeth checked thoroughly.

UNCONSCIOUSNESS

CAUTION

- Do not try to make the victim stand or sit.

- Do not try to feed the victim water, alcoholic beverage or fluid of any kind.

TREATMENT

1. Call a doctor or an ambulance immediately, or bring the victim to a hospital or a doctor.

2. Keep the victim lying flat on his back.

3. Loosen tight clothes, particularly collar and belt. In a female victim, a tight brassiere and/or girdle should be removed.

4. Turn head to side. *See Figure 101 on page 209.*

5. The first-aider should check the victim's personal articles to see if a health card, *see page 28*, is on the victim's person.

If the victim is not breathing

Apply mouth-to-mouth resuscitation. *See page 102.*

What the Doctor Says   There are many causes of

unconsciousness, and the first-aider may not be able to determine the cause. It may be a simple case of fainting, and the victim will recover consciousness in a few minutes without more ado and with no harmful results. However, if the victim does not recover, the first-aider might check the following:

(a) Bleeding.   *See page 47.*
(b) Shock.   *See page 334.*
(c) Head injury.   *See page 287.*
(d) Asphyxiation.   *See page 99.*
(e) Diabetic coma. *See page 184.*
(f) Insulin shock. *See page 298.*

While the above list does not exhaust all the causes for unconsciousness, these are the only matters where a check by the first-aider may be helpful.

First aid should be limited to a few things which can do no harm. Trying to force alcoholic beverage into the mouth of an unconscious victim may cause it to flow into his lungs and tend to drown him.

It is not helpful to try to make the victim sit or stand. This will only allow the tongue to drop back and prevent his breathing. Instead, hold his head back, *see Figure 63 on page 101,* and keep the air passageways open. Turning the head to the side at the same time will allow any kind of fluid to flow out of his mouth and not clog his lungs. *See Figure 101 on page 209.*

Keep the eyelids closed to avoid irritation of the

eyeball. If the eyelids tend to stay open, hold them closed with adhesive tape. *See Figure 100 on page 206.*

The victim may vomit. If this material enters the lungs, pneumonia may develop. That is why it is advisable to turn the head to the side to permit the substance to drain off away from the windpipe.

VEIN RUPTURE

TREATMENT

1. Lay the victim flat on the ground immediately.

2. Place a clean cloth such as a handkerchief or a sterile dressing to the bleeding area, and apply firm pressure. If no material is available, apply pressure with the bare hand. *See page 47* on HOW TO CONTROL BLEEDING.

3. Bandage the wound firmly in place.

4. Seek medical assistance.

What the Doctor Says   If a victim is suffering from severe varicose veins of the leg, one of the bulging veins may rupture spontaneously, or as a result of an injury. If immediate action is not taken, rapid bleeding may prove fatal.

Blood pressure in the veins of a leg is higher when the individual stands erect. Laying the victim flat markedly reduces the pressure, and slows the blood flow. Direct pressure at the bleeding point stops the flow of blood.

Correction of varicose veins by injection, ligation, or stripping will eliminate the danger of rupture.

WHIPLASH

Definition   A wrenching injury of the neck, usually incurred as the result of an auto accident.

Symptoms   Neck pain, limited range of motion, muscle spasms, and headaches.

TREATMENT

1. Wrap a scarf or cloth around the neck to form a thick, wide, encircling support. *See Figure 119, page 262.* This is the same emergency treatment applied in the case of a possible fractured neck.

2. Arrange for further medical care, including X-rays of the neck.

3. Give pain-relieving medicine if available.

What the Doctor Says   Not infrequently, when the neck is severely strained in an accident, the victim becomes momentarily unconscious, or acts stunned, as if he had been hit on the head with a club. Pains in the neck may develop immediately, or may appear in a matter of hours or days. Headaches and shooting pains in the shoulders and upper extremities may also become evident, as may spasms of the neck muscles.

X-ray examination, a collar, sedation, and muscle relaxants will be necessary. Rest is extremely important. About 90% of whiplash victims recover with little or no residual symptoms.

WOUNDS AND LACERATIONS

Definition   Any laceration, incision, or puncture of the skin which causes the victim to bleed. *See Figure 133 and Figure 134.* Open wounds may vary from a clean, small laceration, such as a cut made by a razor blade, to a severe, crushing, bleeding wound associated with an open fracture.

CAUTION

- Do not put merthiolate, zephirin, carbolic acid, alcohol, or any strong antiseptic on an open wound.

TREATMENT

If the bleeding is not serious

1. Apply a sterile gauze dressing. If no sterile dressing is available, use any clean piece of cloth, such as a clean handkerchief, or a clean piece of a freshly laundered sheet. In a dire emergency, even the clean part of a shirt or part of a clean petticoat may be used.

2. Hold the dressing in place with a roller bandage. *See Figure 2, number 8, on page 33.*

If the bleeding is serious

See page 47 on HOW TO CONTROL BLEEDING.

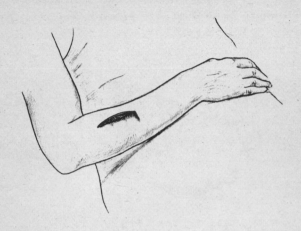

FIG. 133   *INCISED WOUND*   There is a clean, smooth, regular cut in the flesh.

What the Doctor Says   There is a common tendency to disinfect wounds. Don't do it. Do not pour an antiseptic into the wound no matter how contaminated the wound seems to be. Wounds heavily contaminated with dirt, gravel, or grease will require cleansing under anesthesia in an operating room where the surgeon will tidy up a wound by removal of all dead tissue and dirt, and by irrigating the wound with a sterile solution. Each case requires evaluation and treatment by a surgeon.

While venous bleeding will ooze out in a smooth flow, arterial bleeding, always more serious, will be recognized by the intermittent, pulsating spouting of blood. Arterial bleeding may require the application of a tourniquet. *See text on page 51 and accompanying figures.*

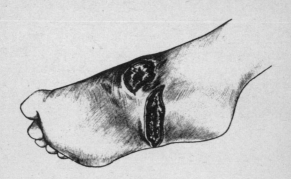

FIG. 134 *LACERATION There are two irregular gashes in the foot. Such a wound could be caused by stepping on a sharp object with irregular surface, such as glass.*

INDEX

Boldface numbers refer to illustrations

367

371

198, 302
  in newborn baby, 177
  with external cardiac
    massage, 107, **108**
mouth-to-nose breathing
    (resuscitation), **104**, 105-
    106, **105**
mouth, **234**, 350
  cleaning out, 102
  frothing at, 181, 199
  -gag, 34
  secretions from, 188, 191,
    353
moving victim, 21, 86, 87, 90,
    130, 131, 133, 142, 155,
    157, 193, 195, 196, **197**,
    237, 240, 261, 263, 275,
    276, 294, 307, 308, 310,
    352, 361
movement, body
  lack of, 193, 212, 301, *see
    also* paralysis
  of victim, 113, 139, 141,
    192, 199, 214, 236, 277,
    362
muscle, 124, 342
  relaxant, 363
  spasms, 181, 199, 330, 345,
    362
  tight, 343
myasthenia gravis, 29

-gas, 308, 309, 343
neck, 24, 116
  bandage for, 60
  bulging vein, 350
  collar, 261, 262, 263, 362,
    363
  fracture of, 261-263, 362
  incision in, 116-117, **116,
    117**
  pain in, 263, 362
  pulse in, 43, **44**, 100, 109,
    111
  splint for, 38, 88
needle, sterilized, 340
Neosporin, 35, 59, 135, 156,
    338
nerve, 118, 277, 302
neurosis, *see* psychiatric
    disturbance
non-conductor of electricity,
    196
nose
  -bleed, 305
  fluids from, 188
  foreign object in, 230
  frostbitten, 285, 286
  infection, 305
  nostrils, 210, 230, 305
  stuffed, 223
numbness, 224, 284, 286

N

narcotic, 100, 357
nasal congestion, 223
nausea, 123, 186, 220, 222,
    223, 289, 295, 308, 329,
    334

O

octopus sting, 346
open fracture, *see* fracture,
    open
ophthalmologist, 205, 207,
    229

382